Neglected Children:
Issues and Dilemma

WORKING TOGETHER FOR CHILDREN,
YOUNG PEOPLE AND THEIR FAMILIES

SERIES EDITOR: PROFESSOR OLIVE STEVENSON

Neglected Children: Issues and Dilemmas

Olive Stevenson
Professor Emeritus of Social Work Studies

**Blackwell
Science**

© 1998 by
Blackwell Science Ltd
Editorial Offices:
Osney Mead, Oxford OX2 0EL
25 John Street, London WC1N 2BL
23 Ainslie Place, Edinburgh EH3 6AJ
350 Main Street, Malden
  MA 02148 5018, USA
54 University Street, Carlton
  Victoria 3053, Australia
10, rue Casimir Delavigne
  75006 Paris, France

Other Editorial Offices:

Blackwell Wissenschafts-Verlag GmbH
Kurfürstendamm 57
10707 Berlin, Germany

Blackwell Science KK
MG Kodenmacho Building
7–10 Kodenmacho Nihombashi
Chuo-ku, Tokyo 104, Japan

The right of the Author to be identified as
the Author of this Work has been asserted
in accordance with the Copyright, Designs
and Patents Act 1988.

First published 1998

Set in 10/12 pt Sabon
by DP Photosetting, Aylesbury, Bucks
Printed and bound in Great Britain by
MPG Books Limited, Bodmin, Cornwall

The Blackwell Science logo is a trade mark
of Blackwell Science Ltd, registered at the
United Kingdom Trade Marks Registry

DISTRIBUTORS

Marston Book Services Ltd
PO Box 269
Abingdon
Oxon OX14 4YN
(*Orders:* Tel: 01235 465500
          Fax: 01235 465555)

USA
Blackwell Science, Inc.
Commerce Place
350 Main Street
Malden, MA 02148 5018
(*Orders:* Tel: 800 759 6102
               781 388 8250
           Fax: 781 388 8255)

Canada
Login Brothers Book Company
324 Saulteaux Crescent
Winnipeg, Manitoba R3J 3T2
(*Orders:* Tel: 204 224-4068)

Australia
Blackwell Science Pty Ltd
54 University Street
Carlton, Victoria 3053
(*Orders:* Tel: 03 9347 0300
           Fax: 03 9347 5001)

A catalogue record for this title
is available from the British Library

ISBN 0-632-04146-3

Library of Congress
Cataloging-in-Publication Data
Stevenson, Olive.
    Neglected children: issues and
dilemmas/Olive Stevenson.
        p. cm.—(Working together for
children, young people, and their
families)
    Includes bibliographical references
and index.
    ISBN 0-632-04146-3
    1. Child welfare—Great Britain.
    2. Family social work—Great Britain.
I. Title. II. Series.
HV751.A6S67 1998
362.76′0941—dc21   97-52985
                                 CIP

To the memory of my
parents who cherished me

Contents

Foreword
Penny Thompson

Executive Director
Sheffield City Council – Social Services

This book should be of interest and relevance to practitioners and managers alike. Not only does it comprehensively review the literature and research on children who are neglected, it also has practical applications. It provides the reader with evidence from practice of interventions that are helpful, not to say essential, when seeking to improve the outcomes for this group of children.

Seeking first to understand the historical, social, economic, parenting factors in children who are neglected, and then those issues less commonly dwelt upon, such as mothers' health, the book draws the reader's attention to the importance of valid and thorough ongoing assessment and planning to build on strengths but also meet children's timescales.

Social work today is conscious of the need to develop evidence based practice. There is a commitment to learning from outcomes and to learning from research. We only have to consider the impact of the publication of *Messages from Research* (Department of Health) and *Assessing Outcomes in Child Care* to recognise the impact of research and policy practice and management in the last five years. Of course there is a long way to go.

This book provides an invaluable contribution to the development of an appreciation of the role of research and learning from practice, and provides approaches for practical application.

Any social worker or social work manager, not to mention health visitor, police officer, teacher, community paediatrician, will recognise the portrait of children who are neglected and will recognise the devastating impact of neglect on healthy development. In many ways, this cohort of children provide the most intractable dilemmas for practice and management and the most telling representation of the effects of social exclusion and poverty. Olive Stevenson has at one and the same time addressed these wider strategic economic and social issues and yet also provided an analysis for practice; no mean feat.

When reading this book I was reminded of my experience as a young and inexperienced social worker in the mid 1970s, working with families whose children showed many of the characteristics of those portrayed in this book. In vain, my co-worker and I struggled for a framework within which to work with these children and their families. We resorted to the development of our own set of 'indices of progress' against which we would chart the progress of children in families. How much we would have benefited from the research and the practical analysis offered by this book for an effective response to these children and families.

Finally, in commending this book I would want to drawn attention to the hard work and dedication of thoughtful practitioners and policy makers whose work on assessment and planning to meet children's needs has contributed to the examples for practice in this book. Their contribution goes beyond making an impact on the lives of individual children, to leaving a very tangible legacy of thinking and practice based tools for application for work with children and families.

Working with Olive Stevenson in Nottinghamshire was a privilege and a sound learning experience. This book provides the reader with the benefit of considerable learning and its impact should be felt by children and families who benefit from a thoughtful appropriate timely and thorough response to their needs.

Preface

This book has been written at the same time as some modest experimental work in Nottinghamshire with neglectful families has been undertaken, supported by the Area Child Protection Committee. A small number of families in which there were serious problems of neglect were identified, with a view to improving interdisciplinary assessment and intervention through a process of consultation. This work is ongoing and for reasons of timing and of confidentiality, it has not been possible to use this experience directly in the book.

However, what I have learnt from this and from the comments of those who are involved has been most significant in the emphasis given, and arguments adduced in this book. Whatever its limitations, and there are many, I am confident that the issues addressed greatly worry those in Britain who work with seriously neglectful families. They would recognise this description.

Paula Simmons is 25. She has three children, Alan aged 8, Mary 3 and Kevin 18 months. The children have different fathers and there is no man currently living in the household. Paula has been known to social services since she was a child; she was in care for short periods and was known to be neglected as a child, and sexually abused in her teens by her stepfather.

There is serious concern about Paula's capacity to offer adequate care to the children. Alan is already known as a budding delinquent in the neighbourhood. His school attendance is erratic and he has been excluded for indiscipline several times. He is teased and bullied by his peers because of his poor clothing and unkempt appearance. He is below average in attainment. Paula cannot offer him effective control and he is often out late in the evening. He is a healthy boy of average intelligence but seems an angry child and shows little warmth to his mother.

Mary seems a rather miserable child. She attends a family centre and frequently arrives smelly and seemingly hungry, often with a runny nose and a skin rash. Her general development, physical and intellectual, is delayed and she has a marked squint. There has been concern that she has not been taken to hospital appointments about this. She constantly seeks affection and reassurance and is very jealous of younger children.

Kevin was a premature baby and was a very difficult baby to feed. He is very passive. During infancy, there was doubt as to whether he was appropriately stimulated.

Paula takes little care of her appearance and often appears tired, dispirited and 'flat' with little interest in responding to the children. She struggles to manage financially and is in debt to 'loan sharks' in the area. She is not well physically, often complaining of heavy periods but is frightened of going to the doctor, in case 'something bad' is found to be the matter. She welcomes visits from health visitors and social workers and will talk at length about the many difficulties which she encounters. She struggles to keep up with the housework and there are times when standards get worryingly low, with flea infestation, unwashed crockery and clothes and a very dirty toilet. Her own personal hygiene is poor.

Those who visit become fond of her. They see a woman who is struggling to survive in very difficult circumstances and who needs much support. However, the quality of life for the children does not seem acceptable, no matter what efforts are made to help. They are not receiving 'good enough' physical care, supervision, control and warmth to ensure their proper development. Health visitors and social workers have put a lot of time and energy with a range of services, into this family. But now they are anxious and uncertain what to do.

What follows is intended to help those who care and worry about such families.

Acknowledgements

I am indebted to many more people and to a far greater extent than is customary for an author. Because this book attempts to bring together material from a wide variety of sources, both from literature and from the professional and academic experience of friends and colleagues, I have unashamedly begged and borrowed (but not, I hope, stolen) from many people, not all of whom I can name here. My thanks to them are no less warm, including those whose work forms an important part of the appendices.

Included in those thanks are all those who attended the Leverhulme workshops in Oxford and Nottingham in 1997 whose names are listed in the Appendix. It was particularly valuable and pleasant to have colleagues from Israel at these events. These interdisciplinary events were an invaluable mechanism for testing out ideas with a wide range of skilled and experienced persons. I am very grateful to the Leverhulme Trust for funding these events.

During this period in which the book was conceived and written, I was Chair of the Nottinghamshire Area Child Protection Committee, the members of which supported me in the idea and gave tangible help in developing action research in the area of neglect. Members were enthusiastically backed in this by staff of the Social Service Department, whose personal help to me has been most generous. In particular, I thank Barbara Cruden, Penny Thompson, John Thorn and Doug Vivyan. I have also sought advice and received help well beyond the call of duty from David Spicer, on the complex issues which neglect raises for the judicial process.

Others whom I particularly wish to thank are: Vicky Bailey, Kwame Owusu-Bempah, Len Smith, June Thoburn, Jane Tresidder and Harriet Ward. Also Karen Nevard at the NSPCC library, whose speedy help in providing material for me was invaluable.

Finally, special thanks to Sara Glennie, who has supported and advised me throughout and to Sarah Jones whose diligence, competence and cheerfulness in the preparation of the manuscript has been a huge comfort.

Chapter 1

What's the Problem?

Introduction

This is a book which I have to write. For the past few years, I have become increasingly aware of a burden in my head which will not go away until it is transferred to paper. Put very simply, the puzzle is this. Professionals agree that neglect as an aspect of child abuse is not at present satisfactorily handled by British child protection services; many also know that there is quite strong evidence that the longer term effects of neglect on children may be even more serious than sporadic physical injury as a result of abuse. Yet, somehow, the nettle has not been grasped. Assessment and protection plans have been less effective than for physical abuse. It is widely acknowledged that professionals may feel a sense of relief when there is an 'incident' or a 'happening' in a particular family (whether of sexual or physical abuse), which is seen to legitimate action for children about whom neglect has long been a primary concern. In what follows, I shall discuss the reasons for the difficulties both professional and academic in addressing the issue and make some suggestions of ways forward.

This introductory chapter identifies problems. Much of the rest of the book explores these problems in greater depth. For this reason, I have largely avoided the rather irritating authors' habit of referring the reader to later chapters.

Those reading this book who work, in whatever capacity, with such families and their children, will have no trouble in conjuring up in their minds the children of whom I am writing. I certainly can. Perhaps these mental pictures will help to keep us focused as complex issues are addressed. Not long ago, I was speaking to a middle aged woman who told me how vividly she recalled, at the age of 5, the little classmate who always arrived at school smelly and with dirty knickers. 'The first thing the class teacher did was to give her a wash and clean knickers.' To me, the striking thing was that the memory was so fresh, showing the impact that one child, somehow 'different', made on other children. Neglect is not, of course, only about physical and external matters. But the example reminds us that in the families we shall be considering, there is usually a sense of social distance from others and an awareness of difference which in turn provokes reactions in the family members and the community within which they are located: in truth, a vicious circle.

Between 1992 and 1995, I directed a research project designed to elicit the perceptions of social workers and the factors which influenced their judgements in cases of neglect and sexual abuse. Cases were discussed in depth with them. The passage below is from an 'open letter' to the social workers who participated in this research and formed part of the feedback to them (Allsopp & Stevenson 1995).

'We felt that they were a representative sample of those cases which had been least straightforward and most thought-provoking and that what these cases had in common might be pointers to your difficulties.

First, these were families mostly living in extreme poverty, in which the basic physical care of children was lacking, the few exceptions involving problems in childcare of a more emotional nature, perhaps the fitful nature of parental attention involved in bout drinking. Family circumstances were often described as "chaotic" and children as "unsupervised" and "understimulated, often being left alone for long periods". Your accounts suggested children who were sad and anxious, at least part of the time, often displaying this in aggression, social withdrawal or nocturnal enuresis; children who were developing poorly, both physically and educationally and seemed particularly vulnerable to physical accidents, or sexual molestation by outsiders. The concerns were for the present welfare and quality of life of these children, though there was an edge of anxiety about their physical safety.

Second, the parents of these children were mostly single and mostly women, often with one or more of a range of problems from some learning difficulties, physical or mental health problems, to alcohol abuse and drug addiction. It seemed that almost none were sadistically neglectful. If the quality of their parenting was poor enough to acquire this label, their disadvantages were such as to mitigate the full weight of moral, let alone legal responsibility, for it. This was a sad omission by people whose life experiences and circumstances could be thought of as equipping them for very little else.

Third, these were nearly all families who had a long relationship with social services, sometimes over three generations. Although they were currently clients or the families of clients under Part 2 of The Children Act, they resembled and, in some cases, were the traditional long term, or revolving door clients, of the old child welfare departments. So it seemed to us, that as Howe (1992) put it, the question: "how can this child be treated?" has become "how can this child be saved?". These welfare cases had been reframed under a system whose rhetoric was safety, protection, purposeful intervention and change to reduce risk. Nevertheless, to an outside observer, it seemed, in fact, that what was being offered to most of the families you discussed was long term state support and supplementary care. This might be interspersed with case closure, but it seemed that 'an incident' might re-establish the relationship. As one social worker remarked of an alcoholic mother, "she's like the poor, she's always with us". Another senior social worker (SSW) referring to a drug addict mother locked in a duty of care to her children, spoke of her as having "a constant burden". We felt that this epithet could in some ways be transferred to him and his department: that, in spite of the rhetoric of parental responsibility of the new Act, the culture of consumerism and the anxiety about dependency and drift that some of you expressed, this welfarist, indeed paternalistic, sense of a duty of care remained.

Fourth, in the majority of the cases that you brought, the parenting was hovering on the edge of "not good enough". There were a few heartening examples of positive change and case closure, but, in general, the problem seemed to be the age-old one of whether and how to change this supportive relationship with parents to a more coercive one through a care order and whether to leave children at home, or (later) to rehabilitate them We felt that, in spite of local authority ideals, under the new Act, of the provision of a spectrum of services to children and families which could be used flexibly under the law to meet need as well as of the continuity of partnership with parents under both voluntary and statutory provision, the acts of "going for an order" or removing children from their parents were still watershed decisions for you all and ones around which the expression of your dilemmas was largely organised.'

(pp. 14–15)

This, I believe, is a fair description of the way many social workers and, indeed, other closely involved professionals, perceive the cases of neglect with which they have to deal. The anxiety and discomfort underlying the ways in which these cases were discussed have been one of the motives for writing this book.

Definitions: arguments and limitations

This book is mainly about *sustained* neglect of children in certain dimensions of their lives. Such neglect may be over a long period or it may occur in episodes or 'bad patches' in parents' lives causing harm to children's development. The notion of neglect does not have to extend to the 'acts of omission' for which ordinary good parents know they are sometimes responsible.

Nor shall I consider in depth the issues which the problem of neglect raises concerning early detection and remedial, 'preventative' work. As this book is being written, the 'refocusing initiative' is high on the agenda of central government policy and of social services departments' activity. The re-affirmation of the importance of family support and of provision to children in need offers a positive approach to intervening constructively with families in difficulties and is particularly relevant to cases of potential or developing neglect. Indeed, in policy terms, there is a case for concentrating effort in that sphere, since, as we shall see, the evidence for success in intervention when there is serious neglect is shaky. Nonetheless, the moral and economic arguments for improving the quality of help offered to seriously neglectful families are unassailable. Although the emphasis of the present policy has great merit, there is a danger that less concentration on the complex and intractable aspects of child protection work may lead to yet further 'neglect of serious neglect'. Such cases are small in number but in terms of human misery, professional time and energy, long term damage and long term costs, their significance is disproportionate.

The definition here is that used by the Nottinghamshire Area Child Protection Committee, similar (though not identical) to many others and to that given in *Working Together* (Department of Health 1989).

> 'A severe and persistent lack of attention to the child's basic needs resulting in significant harmful impairment of health and development or the avoidable exposure of a child to serious danger, including cold or starvation. (This includes abandoned babies/children and those who have been medically diagnosed as non organic failure to thrive.)'

The phrase 'lack of attention to basic needs' in these procedures is the basis for describing different types of abuse.

'Children who are:

- Not receiving adequate food consistent with their potential growth
- Exposed, through lack of supervision, to injuries, including ingestion of drugs or toxic substances
- Exposed to an inadequate dirty and/or cold environment
- Left in "circumstances" without appropriate adult supervision so as to endanger them
- Whose parents/carers are failing or refusing to seek medical advice or treatment'

(Nottingham ACPC Child Protection Procedures 1997)

Two of the above criteria identify lack of supervision as a significant element in considering neglect; failure to seek medical advice or treatment is also specified. Despite this, reports and descriptions of neglect more often focus on the more tangible signs of poor hygiene or food.

Here it is argued that it is equally important to examine the parents' ability to protect their children from physical and emotional hazards and from untreated medical conditions. Furthermore, the reference to lack of 'appropriate supervision' means much more than the occasional 'left alone in the house' incident. There is a very real danger, which I have discussed elsewhere (Stevenson 1996) that, if multiple minor 'accidents' cannot be conclusively established as intentional abuse, they are discounted: whereas, they may be indicative of quite inadequate parental supervision *or* abuse, both of which must be taken seriously. This was graphically illustrated in the inquiry into the death of Stephanie Fox (Lynch & Stevenson 1990) in which a total of 27 minor injuries, many to the head, were recorded to Stephanie and her siblings in the last 2 years of her life, and the number increased markedly in the last 6 months of Stephanie's life. Argument concerning parental 'intention' may simply deflect us from effective appraisal of the parents' ability to provide a safe enough environment for the child.

Even if neglect is construed more widely in terms of the physical effects of 'omissions of care', we are still left with a basic illogicality in attempting to distinguish between physical, emotional, social and intellectual aspects of abuse. Neglect is not, and cannot be about, only physical matters because children's needs do not come in strictly divided compartments. The younger the child, the more all aspects of his/her development are intertwined. It has been argued that 'emotional abuse' is difficult to define and that 'neglect' is in some way less problematic because it can focus upon observable physical matters. The irony of that argument is that there is plenty of evidence that the existence of 'physical neglect' itself has not been viewed with sufficient understanding or precision to enable appropriate action to be taken.

The word 'maltreatment' is often used to cover both neglect and abuse, and avoids the awkwardness of distinguishing between acts of omission (neglect) and acts of commission (abuse). Furthermore, the phrase 'neglect and emotional abuse' often puts the two elements together. The position taken in this book is that all neglect constitutes a form of emotional abuse because of the importance of addressing children's needs holistically. However, there are some forms of emotional abuse, such as verbal sadism, which cannot be described as 'neglect' without straining the term too far.

Recent research undertaken by Glaser, Prior and Lynch on emotional abuse confirms the importance of keeping these two aspects of maltreatment linked in the minds of those in child protection work (Glaser & Prior 1997). Glaser and colleagues investigated 94 children from 56 families; 54% of these children were registered under the sole category of emotional abuse and 48% were registered jointly for emotional abuse and one or more categories of abuse or neglect. The mean age of the children at registration was 7 years 5 months, but nearly all had been known to social services departments for varying lengths of time, some substantial. Most of the forms of ill treatment to which the children had been subjected are highly significant in relation to consideration of neglect; for example, 27% were found to have been emotionally abused through 'emotional unavailability or neglect' 34% through 'denigration or rejection' and 42% through 'developmentally inappropriate interaction with the child'.

The more one probes the definitions and distinctions between emotional abuse and neglect the less satisfactory they become. When neglect is construed as an omission of care, which affects not only physical but social, intellectual and emotional development, the association between the two becomes clear. For example, if an infant is said to have 'dirtied his nappy on purpose' and is left unchanged, this may be due to 'developmentally inappropriate' expectations but it leads to neglect of physical care. If a 6 year old is required to undertake tasks (or roles) for which he/she is too young and adult/child boundaries are blurred, this may lead to neglect of his/her social, intellectual and emotional needs *as a 6 year old* (for play, cuddles, etc.). We may well have reached a stage when clarification and reshaping of these categories are appropriate. Meanwhile, however, whatever the wider ramifications, there is much work to be done to address more systematically those aspects of maltreatment in which omission of care places well-being and development in jeopardy.

One important issue which arises in any discussion of the nature of neglect or emotional abuse is the significance of cultural factors in the definition of the problem. (This matter is explored at some length in Chapter 4.) Whilst in no way minimising the intrinsic interest and importance of cultural factors in approaching families where neglect is the subject of concern, such debates should not divert us from a recognition that there is a very significant cross cultural consensus about the basic needs for healthy child development. To the extent that cultural factors are 'a problem' in addressing neglect, it may be as much about the approach and anxieties of workers as about the definition of serious neglect itself.

Neglect, then, covers a wide range of behaviours, including those involving poor physical care and those involving lack of supervision or control. As Crittenden (1993) comments 'it is unlikely that neglect is a unitary condition' (p. 28). Thus, one would not expect to be able to make generalisations about the characteristics of all seriously neglectful parents. Such parents and caregivers are not a homogeneous group, even if they are seen as distinctive in terms of the grave concerns which they raise about their parenting capacity. Furthermore, since neglect is not infrequently associated with other kinds of maltreatment, especially physical abuse, the characteristics or behaviour of such parents will not necessarily be particular to that group. Many of the difficulties, such as high levels of domestic, 'spousal' abuse, will be found more generally.

We do not therefore seek a 'neglectful parents syndrome', within which understanding can be conveniently packaged, although there may be certain aspects of neglectful behaviour which can be helpfully viewed from particular theoretical perspective. 'Neglect' has been chosen for the focus of this book, quite simply, because it worries many professionals who believe that children's health, well-being and development in such situations has been seriously damaged and inadequately protected by those in business to do so.

Thresholds

The word 'thresholds' is much used in the field of child protection. The only relevant definition in the *Oxford English Dictionary* is 'entrance'. Entrance to what, one may ask? In current usage, it implies that we have reached a critical moment when we may need to take further steps to protect a child. To do so we will always have to assess the well-being of the child and often have to assess the capacity of a parent to offer improved care.

In contemporary British child welfare, there are likely to be three main 'thresholds' in cases of neglect, in each of which the judgements made in both domains, i.e. children's well-being and parental capacity, may be crucial. The first is when there are found to be some elements of neglect but, rather than a child protection plan, services to the family on the basis of 'children in need' are the appropriate response. The second is when the neglect is so serious that the children need to be protected by registration and the services associated with the child protection system. Third, there is the threshold when it is necessary to take court action, which may lead to removal of the children from their families. This book seeks to explore the possibility of establishing a systematic approach to the assessment of children's well-being at any stage in the process. It is particularly important that the approach should facilitate ongoing review of children to monitor improvements or deterioration in their situation, to facilitate movement between the legislative categories of 'in need' and 'in need of protection' and to reach decisions that the children are no longer safe at home, *because of neglect*. Examination of files and records, sometimes, sadly, after a child has died, often shows that there is no coherent picture of a child's state over time. Disconnected observations do not address the vital question; put crudely, is the child and the care he or she is receiving getting better or worse?

Here, however, we hit a problem which has exercised me greatly in the preparation of this book. The word 'thresholds' brings to mind the idea of measurement; 'measurement' suggests the need for accuracy and validity in the tests applied. It is a short step from this to the kinds of questionnaires, check lists and forms which many workers at field level have come to dread and resent, not least in the area of child protection, in which failure to complete relevant documentation may attract serious criticism. The American literature on neglect and maltreatment is replete with references to a range of tests available on attitudes to neglectful parents, parenting capacity and child development. In this country, the work of Rutter (1967, 1968) on factors involved in assessing emotional and psychiatric disorders in children has been widely used within education; Minty and Patterson (1994) have worked on an instrument for demonstrating neglect (Appendix IV). Whilst it will be useful to have some specialised and validated 'in depth' tests available for particular purposes, it seems important to utilise a general framework which will identify the broad parameters within which neglect can be assessed but which has the potential for more detailed analysis when that is appropriate.

Social service departments are familiar with the *Looking after Children* materials prepared by Dartington Research Unit and others, to assess the well-being of children being cared for by the local authority, away from their parents (Appendix IX). Indeed, the impact of this work is already evident in relation to children in their own families. For example, Nottinghamshire Social Services Department has prepared a form for a second stage assessment (Appendix VIII) which utilises six of the dimensions of the *Looking After Children* material for this purpose. The seven dimensions of children's well-being are:

• Health
• Education
• Identity
• Family and social relationships
• Emotional and behavioural development
• Self presentation
• Self care skills

It is suggested that these dimensions should be the focus for consideration of 'thresholds' for two reasons. First, they have been most carefully developed and can be assumed to represent a contemporary consensus about the elements necessary to consider in children's welfare. This consensus extends beyond professionals to 'ordinary' parents, whose views of the acceptability of the criteria were also obtained (Ward 1995). Second, the material is by now relatively familiar at least to workers in social services departments. (The extent to which other workers have been involved in their day to day use is not yet clear.) This will make it relatively easier to influence practice.

However, although there is a strong case for making use of the general framework, it does not solve three of the difficulties in determining 'thresholds' in cases of neglect. First, when they are used for 'looked after children', they will pinpoint certain 'omissions' in the children's care and will give clear indications of where action is needed. But they are rarely used for the measurement of well-being. Furthermore, the construction of the materials, in which all seven dimensions are assessed according to the age and stage of the child, has led to very detailed forms which some workers have found onerous. (It must be added that their relevance and sensitivity has been generally appreciated and this no doubt helps to overcome resistance.) There is, however, a substantial difference between their use for individual children being cared for in the 'official' system and for children in neglectful families; often there are several children at home and, inevitably, assessment depends in part on parental accounts, which are likely to be variable in reliability. A third difficulty is that they are only concerned with the children's well-being, not with an assessment of parenting capacity. Clearly, this raises problems in some situations: 'significant harm' may be demonstrated but the second element in the legislative process requires parental responsibility for it to be identified. However, once parental responsibility for neglect is agreed to be the problem, it is much easier to attribute to parental shortcomings than in some cases of physical abuse or sexual abuse, since it usually involves omission of care over a considerable period of time.

These difficulties do not, in my view, override the advantages in using this general framework, but they do suggest the need for a rather blunter instrument than many academics and perfectionists may wish! It seems more important to develop *a way of looking* at neglectful families, based on a sound consensus concerning child development, which can be used systematically at different points but which does not impose unrealistic burdens on field workers. Furthermore, as the authors of the materials have themselves pointed out (Ward 1995), the very fact that such guidance exists serves a more general purpose in raising awareness of the needs of particular groups of children, in our case, of neglected children.

Neglect in context

This chapter is entitled *What's the Problem?* So far, the discussion has focused on the notion of neglect as a category of maltreatment. But, as I have argued elsewhere, (Stevenson 1996) the failures to tackle the problem adequately go further and are, in some ways, deeper than these conceptual difficulties. It would be naive, therefore, to hope for significant improvement in work with neglectful families without seeking to understand and hence to modify some of the existing contextual difficulties.

In common with other work with people in difficulty, there is a confusion and fear at the heart of this debate. The injunction to 'condemn the sin and not the sinner' has been at the centre of the ethical framework for social work for many years. It is, of course, extremely difficult to preserve this distinction. There is a deep rooted feeling that by attributing difficulties, in part at least, to the behaviour of the person concerned, one is blaming them. There is, of course, a way round that, if it can be shown that the difficulties (say, in parenting) may be connected to earlier experiences (say, in childhood) over which the parent had no control, or indeed, to basic limitations in ability. Yet that, in turn, leads to increased concern about a model for understanding which appears to diminish personal responsibility. It is felt that is a slippery slope and may encourage dependence, instead of building on strengths. Part of the fear of 'blaming' reflects a legitimate concern that individualistic explanations of deviant behaviour may be used to deflect attention from social deficits and social evils. This is often presented as a dichotomy between the left and the right politically. It can be seen at its most unattractive in the ways in which some of the members of the former Conservative government picked out certain groups, such as lone mothers, for censure. But this places the professionals in an untenable position. They should not have to deny or inhibit their insight into the difficulties of parents for fear of being 'aligned' with the right of politics.

Since 1980, child protection work in the UK has further confused this picture. On the one hand, the sheer emphasis on, and resources devoted to, protecting children from 'dangerous' adults, usually their parents, and on the assessment of risk in individual cases, seemed to reinforce an 'individualistic' model for understanding, indeed, for constructing the very problem, rather than an emphasis on external factors. On the other hand, what has been described as the 'forensic' model of investigation had led to the emphasis on incidents and episodes to which I have earlier referred, rather than on a more holistic approach. This shift has been referred to in terms of 'socio-legal' rather than 'socio-medical' discourse. The former, although it has its place in the range of activities in child abuse investigations, can have a curiously blocking effect on the search for understanding which must precede long term judgements about intervention. Short term decisions may indeed have to be made simply on 'happenings' which place a child at risk. But when we enter the field of intelligent anticipation (not prediction) and the likelihood of future harm is considered, the need for the holistic approach in many cases is demonstrable and essential in cases of neglect. However, the term, 'socio-medical' needs qualification, for it carries with it the baggage of past conflict in the field of child abuse and elsewhere. For a start, it raised fears of domination by two, differing but narrow, approaches which have been influential and controversial. The first, ironically, supported a sociolegal or forensic way of looking at the problem, for it sought to establish precision and reliability in diagnosis. No one can doubt its value given the early resistance of the medical profession to the belief in the existence of 'battered' babies and its utility within the judicial system itself, but its limitations have become increasingly apparent, especially in relation to neglect.

The second approach, epitomised in the work of Kempe (for example, Kempe & Helfer 1968) stressed mental health problems of the parents in the aetiology of child abuse. Again, this has played, and will continue to play, an important part in raising awareness of such connections. But it has also been sharply criticised because of the biased samples on which early studies were based and because the very use of certain psychiatric and psychoanalytic classifications is controversial. The consequences of this approach may, it has been argued, lead to altogether too pessimistic a view of the characteristics of those who abuse their children. Yet whatever terminology we use, and there are difficulties associated with alternatives, we need a phrase to express the holistic ideal which is at the heart of effective and purposeful thought about abusive parents, most particularly neglectful ones. It seems likely, then, that workers have been caught in a kind of pincer movement: from one side, guilt and anxiety about 'blaming' and unease about the use of 'pathological' descriptors; from the other, an organisational context which has discouraged systematic reflections about people, rather than events.

A further difficulty concerns the courts and the judicial process. Work with neglected children and their families often starts well before the involvement of the courts and may never reach them. More effective work with 'children in need' may further reduce the need for courts to be brought into the process. However, it is evident, from what social workers have said that the shadow of the courts hangs, unhelpfully, over their heads when they are confronting serious cases of neglect. This centres on the nature of evidence needed for neglect to be proved. In some ways, this is surprising. Workers are extremely unlikely to take cases to court without grounds for serious concern; there is now an accepted corpus of literature on children's physical, intellectual and emotional needs; nor is it clear that magistrates and judges would be reluctant to make orders on the basis of definite and systematically collected evidence (Minty & Patterson 1994). However, it seems to have become part of the mythology that bringing such cases is fraught with difficulties; some actual horror stories feed the myth. It is important to analyse what lies behind such views and to consider the underlying issues which they raise.

The approach of lawyers to such cases is not generally sympathetic to the nature of the evidence required. Irritation at vagueness or about arguments between 'experts' should not blind lawyers to two facts. First, there is a great deal of knowledge and research concerning children's needs which is *not* contentious, even cross culturally. It affords a sound basis for the consideration of the deficits in the upbringing of neglected children. Second, child development cannot, and should not, be compartmentalised so that physical evidence of neglect is not connected to emotional, social and intellectual harm. This is, quite simply, unsound. It seems that we need a kind of pact between the workers and experts on the one hand and the lawyers and the magistrates on the other, so that, if the evidence the former present is detailed and systematic, based on sound research, the latter will accept a model of evidence which is holistic.

Even if that understanding were to be achieved, however, our difficulties in establishing the concept of neglect within the judicial process would not be over. A further problem lies in the way in which parental roles and responsibilities are viewed. This is not a clear cut division between the groups of professionals and magistrates involved. Rather it reflects a widespread difficulty in reconciling the interests of neglected children with fairness to parents and with the notion of 'partnership with parents'.

Anxiety concerning the courts' response to cases of neglect is not solely in terms of establishing the concept of neglect. It also arises because, in seeking either a supervision or care order, it must be demonstrated that 'the harm is attributable to the care given to the child, or likely to be given to him, if the order were not made, not being what it would be reasonable to expect a parent to give to him; or the child's being beyond parental control' (Section 31, The Children Act 1989). In short, the connection between harm and the parental 'failure' must be demonstrated. This sits uncomfortably in the minds of those who have accepted the broader goal of working in partnership and is particularly difficult in cases of neglect, in contrast to many other cases of abuse, where parental action (rather than inaction) can readily be seen to be unacceptable.

Everyone concerned is aware that, in many cases (though not all), failure to provide good enough care by parents is bound up with their limitations in ability, distressing family backgrounds and mental health problems. When chronic poverty is added to this, there may be a pervasive sense of sympathy, linked to the hope that such parents can be helped to improve their care sufficiently to permit the children to stay at home. The lack of precision concerning the effects of neglect on development plays into the chronic indecision which is so often a feature of work in such cases. Optimism about the potentiality for change must, however, be underpinned by realism and by a reasonable knowledge base about likely and unlikely change and improvement in parenting capacity and the conditions necessary for it.

On this matter there is research, mainly from the USA, which offers some valuable insights, discussed later. Nonetheless, when critical discussions concerning the future of the children have to be taken and the courts are bound to consider the capacity of parents to sustain or improve the existing quality of care, we are in foggier territory than in relation to child development. The overriding imperative that we should seek to work in partnership with parents, linked to uncertainty as to what change or development is possible, has led to some decisions to leave children at home whose quality of life is simply not 'good enough'.

Thus, uncertainties and anxieties surrounding work with neglectful families affect, and are affected by, the judicial process, in reality and as perceived by the professionals concerned, especially the social workers. However, they also connect with the organisational context of social services departments and with interdisciplinary and interagency relationships which are at the heart of so much child protection work.

The shift from 'socio-medical' to 'socio-legal' approaches in child protection has affected the assessment of neglect and has been fundamentally unhelpful because it causes the wrong and less important questions to be asked. It also increases difficulties in communication between health professionals, notably health visitors and paediatricians, whose approach is 'socio-medical', and social workers. Health visitors have been particularly concerned that referrals for neglect have not received the same attention from social workers as those for other forms of abuse. Many professionals are enthusiastic about a shift of paradigm, a different way of looking at abuse, which will encompass neglect more satisfactorily. This 'shift of paradigm' has extensive implications for social work practice. Most particularly, it will require a reappraisal of the nature and extent of intervention in serious cases of neglect. A shortage of resources but also, more elusive but none the less pervasive, a pseudo 'business like' approach had led to an emphasis on short term intervention whenever possible. 'Can we close the case?' has been a question too often asked inappropriately in serious cases of neglect. If we are serious about seeking to sustain or improve parenting in such cases, it may be a long term task, spanning the lives of the children into adulthood. Before such an ideal is dismissed as unrealistic, we must remind ourselves of the costs, first, of the present sporadic activity over years, documented in the files of such families, second, of children in care and, third, of the damage to the next generation of children. Moreover, even if 'the business' cannot be conducted briskly with case closure in view, it can be purposeful; the reaction against the vague and unfocused 'support' of an earlier generation of workers was justifiable. A failure to assess the consequences of neglect has contributed to a lack of direction in much professional activity.

There are two further matters of great significance in understanding the nature of the problem which confronts us. The first concerns the sympathy and compassion which the parents (usually mothers) of neglected children raise in workers, especially health visitors and social workers. So often the parents have themselves been the victims of the same type of upbringing which is currently being criticised. Nor do they provoke the same sense of outrage as some other abusers who inflict very obvious injury on children. (They may, however, contribute to such harm by their failure to protect.) They are struggling with major environmental deficits, of which financial poverty is only one, which make us feel ashamed of the society in which we live. Uncertainty about thresholds interacts, again, with such feelings and may lead to a kind of passivity, on the part of the workers. To act, it seems, is to blame – and who can bear to do so in the miserable circumstances of such parents? One of the social workers in the research to which previous reference was made (Allsopp & Stevenson 1995) described his sympathy with the predicament of the women who were his clients and his anxieties about the role in which he was placed, in which authority (including the courts') had to be exercised to protect the children at times from an alcoholic mother.

> 'I think that women get a rough deal anyway out of society and they have been dumped, they've all been deserted by their men, they've always been used and abused by men all through their lives, their fathers have abused them, their boyfriends/husbands and here we come along, male social workers. We start using and abusing them ... we're punishing them for what society's done to them.'

(Allsopp & Stevenson 1995, p. 34)

The duty (morally as well as legally) to put the neglected children first never requires us to lose sympathy with the understanding of parents; it does, however, require us, on occasion, to act as decisively to protect children as we do in other types of abuse, a fact of which that social worker was well aware.

As if the above were not difficult enough, there is a second strand of particular relevance to social workers at the present time. That is, the loss of confidence in the capacity of the system to provide good enough alternatives to parental care. There is a profound sense of pessimism about present arrangements for 'looking after children'; the extent to which this pessimism is justified cannot be explored here, but it is bound to colour judgements and actions about children neglected in their homes. Again, we are in a vicious circle; the longer children remain at home in unsatisfactory circumstances, the harder it may be for substitute care to be beneficial.

Conclusions

This chapter has argued that :

- Neglect is not a unitary concept but an administrative category, covering a range of behaviours which are characterised by the omission of care.
- Nonetheless, the term neglect describes a group of families who are recognised by professionals as sharing some common characteristics and who cause much anxiety in those workers.
- The links between neglect and emotional abuse are very strong; present categorisation leads to confusion and obscures the inter-

action of physical, social, emotional and intellectual factors in child development.

- A way forward must be found, as a basis for action, including judicial intervention, to provide more precise focused evidence of developmental harm (or improvement). The use of the seven dimensions in the *Looking after Children* materials offers a starting point.

Chapter 2

Approaches to Understanding

This short chapter sets out the framework which I shall use in seeking to understand the phenonomen of neglect, as it was described in the preceding chapter, and in considering purposeful intervention.

The broad outline of the framework is one which is applicable in principle to all work with families where children are 'in need' or need protection. (Indeed it has still wider application.) But the emphasis that is put on the various aspects of family functioning will vary greatly according to the nature of the problems which the families present. As we shall see in the families with which we are here concerned, there are particular difficulties and tensions in balancing and integrating the various factors involved.

The approach chosen here therefore has two strands. First, as Fig. 2.1 illustrates, the widely used 'ecological' model enables us to examine a wide range of factors which affect such parents in common with many others. Second, however, it further enables us to focus on particular factors which research or experience suggest are of especial relevance to the predicament of these families. Thus, for example, Chapter 4 examines the impact of social isolation in the lives of these families.

Figure 2.1 is a stylised and simplistic diagram to indicate a systemic approach to the subject; it suggests that just as family members interact with each other, so the family both collectively and individually relates to the world outside. There are a number of dimensions. First, there is the 'nuclear' family, within which individuals interact. Second, there is the wider family; then there is 'the local community', within which there are a number of groupings, both formal (the professionals, agencies, local government) and informal (friends, neighbours, etc.) and also the environment (shops, roads, etc.). Finally, there is wider society which provides the overarching structures of law and governance, including social policies, and which influences families in all kinds of ways, especially through the media. Families and the individuals within them interact with all these wider systems, both directly, and indirectly through other systems.

This model emphasises a holistic view of family functioning and implies that change and development occur, for better or for worse, in a number of dimensions. It does less than justice, however, to the com-

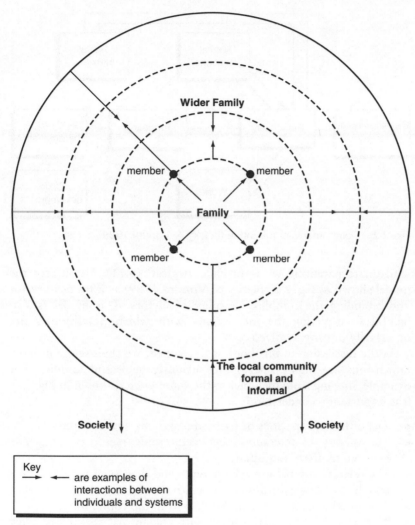

Fig. 2.1 Towards understanding: ecological model.

plex processes by which individuals and families internalise social and cultural norms and values so that the world outside lives in the minds and feelings of those within the family. Thus, for example, at a very early age, children absorb social expectations concerning gender, not only from their parents but also from a wide range of other influences from school to television, to which they are subjected.

Gaudin (1993) describes and summarises the literature concerning wide ranging factors which interact in cases of neglect and concludes that, despite the relative paucity of research on neglect as compared with other kinds of maltreatment, 'it is clear, from existing studies and from the experience of practitioners, that there is no single cause of the

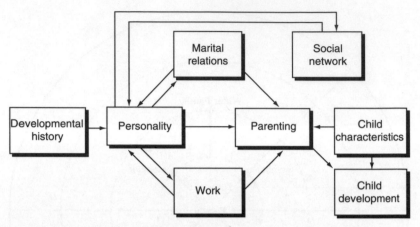

Fig. 2.2   Determinants of parenting (Belsky & Vondra 1989).

inadequate parenting we term child neglect' (p.11). He utilises the model shown in Fig. 2.2 (Belsky & Vondra 1989) as a framework for understanding the complex interplay of factors. This model is also helpful in depicting the interactions with which practitioners are necessarily directly involved.

As the discussion in this book is developed, we shall see that many dimensions are highly relevant to seriously neglectful families. For example, moving from the inner to the outer circles, shown in Fig. 2.1, it is important to understand:

- The differing capacities of particular parents and children.
- The quality of interaction between family members, especially between mothers and infants.
- The relationship between the parents and their own parents which may be highly significant, both positively and negatively.
- The social isolation of such families from the community.
- That the family's relationships with the formal sector are often highly problematic.
- That their practical situation within the local environment is frequently unsatisfactory.
- That their well-being is profoundly affected by social policies, such as those concerning education, social security and employment.

Such an approach, however, does not mean that all such factors can be, or need be, given equal emphasis at a particular point in time, nor that individual workers can or should pay attention to them all. It does, however, imply the need for a co-ordinated strategy which, because of the complex problems such families present, will necessarily involve interprofessional and interagency co-operation at quite a sophisticated level. The families themselves may seem overwhelmed to the point of powerlessness, so the workers may experience similar feelings. The model is useful. Though it is theoretical, it is also very practical; it provides a kind of map to guide us through very confusing terrain. It also fits well into the seven dimensions of children's well-being outlined in the previous chapter. Subsequent chapters will discuss some of these interactions and their impact on the families which are here the focus of our concern.

Chapter 3
Poverty

Introduction

Nearly all the families with which this book is concerned are poor, whether that term is used to describe their financial situation or their overall material quality of life. However, most workers directly involved do not accept that poverty alone creates the difficulties with which they grapple. There is an uneasy tension in the way such matters are discussed of which I also am aware in developing the themes in this book.

In some ways, neglectful families highlight an issue of much wider significance, namely, the ways in which the difficulties and problems of individuals and families are seen and understood by the professionals involved and to what they are attributed. Social workers, in particular, have been at the centre of a struggle between competing theories. Although there are many fierce arguments amongst those who are described as holding 'intra or inter personal' theories, these are not experienced as intensely by less specialised workers as are the tensions *between* those theories and those which are rooted in a structural analysis of people's problems.

It has not proved easy to keep these different approaches in balance and to integrate them in practice. It has sometimes seemed that social workers have been left rudderless, without a sense of direction based on an effectively integrated approach. For example, on the one hand, they have often been accused of giving inadequate attention to poverty (Becker 1997) and, on the other, to the psychosocial perspectives, notably the connections between past and present behaviour (Howe 1996).

Poverty in the context of work with neglectful families

Nowhere is this confusion better illustrated than in the field of work with neglectful families. Not infrequently, the families receive financial help from social services which in aggregate over time is not inconsiderable, in relation to the limited funds available through the use of (the old) Section 1 or (the new) Section 17 provisions (The Children Act 1989).

This was well illustrated in the report on 'Paul' who died as a result of gross neglect (The Bridge Consultancy 1995). The Bridge Consultancy note that:

'considerable amounts of money were provided to the parents to buy furnishings and equipment, which was subsequently sold. We have noted at least three periods when this occurred... Considerable general funding, over many years, was provided by Neighbourhood Services, plus several hundreds of pounds raised by health visitors from charitable trusts, which seemed to have little effect on the family's situation'

(The Bridge Consultancy 1995, p. 152)

Similarly in the course of the review into Stephanie Fox's death (Lynch & Stevenson 1990) it became apparent that nearly £1000 had been paid to the family (in small amounts) during the year preceding Stephanie's death. Yet this type of help may not form part of a co-ordinated plan, may be essentially reactive to family financial crises and rarely seems to improve matters.

On the other side of the picture, the reason for a seriously dirty home is very rarely explored in terms of the message it may be giving about a mother's feelings and the implications for work with her. Instead a 'cleaning up' squad may effect a temporary improvement before the situation again deteriorates. It cannot be too strongly emphasised that an effective assessment and intervention involves recognition of the dynamic interplay of a complex range of factors. However, this is both intellectually and emotionally difficult to manage and is not helped by the 'lobbies' to which workers are exposed, in which one way of seeing the problems may be stressed to the exclusion of others. We cannot here explore the changing and complex effects of such influences. But they are not remote or 'academic'; rather, they pull workers in different directions because, explicitly and implicitly, they modify, challenge or, sometimes, distort the way problems are seen. In this book, I assume poverty to be an extremely significant factor in the lives of the families about whom we worry, but only one in a complex web of factors.

We are fortunate in the UK in having available extensive research and literature on the subject, developed within the discipline of social policy over many years. The distinction between concepts of absolute and relative poverty, different ways of measuring poverty and of viewing its causes – all these and much else have been explored in depth and detail in post war years. There is no doubt that 'neglectful' families suffer gravely, along with many others, from the effects of poverty. They simply cannot 'make ends meet' and the consequent effects on physical and mental health (of adults and children), on quality of life and on self esteem are incalculable. In asserting this, rather than advancing detailed evidence, I am starting from what I believe to be an accepted position of those who are well informed.

The impact of state policies

This takes us to the impact of state policy on the lives of a large number in the general population, amongst whom are 'our' families. The Child Poverty Action Group (CPAG) (Oppenheim & Harker 1996) documents this with admirable clarity. One of the underlying reasons for the anger and dismay amongst workers who have been in the front line for some years has been an awareness of the growth in the numbers of people in poverty and of the inequality between our citizens. CPAG describe this succinctly and powerfully:

'The latest figures show that between 13 and 14 million people – around a quarter of the population in the United Kingdom – were living in poverty measured by either of the two most common definitions. In 1979, less than half that number were living 'in poverty' ... 'In the last decade and a half, the living standards of the poor and the affluent have marched in opposite directions. Between 1979 and 1992/93, the real incomes (after housing costs) of those in the poorest tenth fell by 18%; the average rose by 37% whilst the richest enjoyed a staggering rise of 61%'.

(p. 1)

CPAG further point out that in the same period children have been more vulnerable to poverty than society as a whole. Figure 3.1 illustrates this. CPAG estimate some 4.3 million children – a third of all children – were living in poverty in the early 1990s. Of these, 71% were households with no-one in full-time employment, and within that about 50% were in lone parent families.

Many readers of this book will be ashamed, as I am, that this has happened; indeed, it was, at least in part, responsible for the political upheaval of the May 1997 general election. The introductory chapter of the CPAG publication sums up impressively the impact of poverty on the lives of so many families:

'Poverty means staying at home, often being bored, not seeing friends, not going to the cinema, not going out for a drink and not being able to take the children out for a trip or a treat or a holiday. It means coping with the stresses of managing on very little money, often for months or even years. It means having to withstand the onslaught of society's pressure to consume. It impinges on relationships with others and with yourself. Above all, poverty takes away

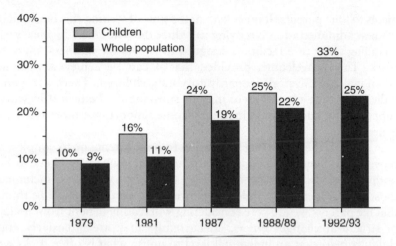

Source. DSS, *Households below Average Income. a statistical analysis. 1979.1988/89* and *1979.1992/93,*and revised edition, HMSO. 1992 and 1995

Fig. 3.1 Proportion of children and population living in poverty between 1979 and 1992/3 (living below 50% average income after housing costs). (*Source:* DSS: *Household below Average Income: a statistical analysis.* 1979–1988/89 and 1979–1992/3, and revised edition. HMSO 1992 and 1995.)

the tools to create the building blocks for the future – your 'life chances'. It steals away the opportunity to have a life unmarked by sickness, a decent education, a secure home and a long retirement. It stops people being able to plan ahead. It stops people being able to take control of their lives'.

(Oppenheim & Harker 1996, p. 5)

Thus, the pervasiveness of poverty, its penetration into every aspect of the lives of individuals and families is apparent. However, it is not surprising that some families manage it better than others. The differing abilities of individuals, particular circumstances which increase stress or complicate daily living, all play a part in producing variable responses to the basic deficit – that 'there isn't enough to go round'.

We help parents who are seriously neglectful of their children if we seek to understand their particular responses to the deplorable material situation in which they are so often placed. Most of these families live in poverty, in common with many others, but they may have other characteristics or difficulties in common too, some of which are pertinent and contribute to their poverty.

The numbers of lone parents have increased more than three fold between 1976 and 1995, when it was estimated at 1 700 000; the proportion receiving income support or its predecessor, supplementary benefit, increased in that period from 36% to 64% (Oppenheim & Harker 1996). It is fair to say that any government, of whatever political colour, would be concerned about such a growth of benefit payments to lone parents. It is evident, at the time of writing this book, that the new administration is moving to reduce these numbers by measures including child care facilities, designed to encourage mothers to go to work. This is welcome, provided that it can be achieved without emotional (or physical) jeopardy to young children. There are some indications that a lone parent may be substantially better off in work supported by family credit than on income support, but more research is needed.

In general, then, whether in relation to lone parents or to couples, a move from 'benefit dependency' towards employment is likely to be both financially and psychologically of benefit to families, including those who neglect their children. However, it would be naive to think that the parents we are here considering will readily benefit from policy or structural changes unless, concurrently, they are intensively and skillfully helped at an individual level to utilise what is offered. As we shall see, such parents are often lacking in confidence, have low esteem and a history of educational failure, which may or may not be associated with intellectual limitations. They may not readily take up new opportunities. Thus, there is even a danger that, if the situation of 'poor parents' generally improves, this particular group will, in the eyes of the general public, begin to stand out negatively from their peers.

Whatever hopes we may have for improving employment opportunities and reducing dependency on state benefits, there will remain a significant proportion of families who need state support; therefore the adequacy of this provision must remain a source of concern. For example, there is a debate about the relative costs of one parent as compared with two parent families. The Social Security Advisory Committee (of which I am a member) decided there was insufficient evidence for concluding, as had the previous government, that a lone parent on income support was overcompensated financially compared with a couple with children (Social Security Advisory Committee 1997). Such arguments can only be resolved by rigorous research; even then, differing assumptions about need upon which calculations are made and which may be equally valid, may lead to different conclusions.

Some benefit matters, however, require the application of principles rather than simply research. One of these, which profoundly affects poor families, is debt. Most of them are in considerable debt; no doubt some would accumulate debts even if they were better supported financially. But over the past decade and a half, there has been a steady shift in official policy towards an acceptance that families in poverty, as defined by the state, can routinely pay back to, or via, the state a substantial amount of their basic income in respect of arrears for essential household services or goods. Deduction at source may be of two kinds. First, they may be made for arrears in payments of housing costs, gas, electricity, water, fines, social fund loans and overpayment of income support. No more than three deductions can be made – in the above order of priority and there are tight limits to the amounts which can be deducted. Second, deductions for current payments for necessities such as electricity and gas may be made. Up to 25% of the total benefit can be taken at source without the claimants' consent.

The Department of Social Security makes plain that it would prefer not to operate a quasi-banking service and would like to end its present role, but others argue that such arrangements are in fact in the claimants' interest – to avoid disconnections and the installation of pre-payment meters which are more expensive. Whatever the advantages of present arrangements, these procedures muffle the protests and public criticisms which would be heard if the families had to do without basic goods and services. But if some families, many of whom will have other debts as well, can have up to 25% of their benefit deducted, the longer term effects of living on an income well below basic subsistence must be serious, especially in relation to nutrition and health. Thus, at 1997 rates, a family of four (one adult and three children) whose total income, excluding housing benefit, is £99.85 per week may receive only £75.00 per week even before other debts are paid.

Although the policy of compulsory deductions may on occasion avoid dire consequences, government policy itself has added to the poverty of some families. As Becker (1997) points out, the introduction of Social Fund loans in the 1980s was 'the first time in post war British social security policy that the poorest claimants have been expected to repay money given to them to meet their exceptional needs' (p. 66). Some have argued that the existence of interest free Social Fund loans provides a better alternative than resort to the commercial sector or loan shark. Whilst this may be so, it is indefensible that the state can deduct up to a quarter of a family's benefit and, in my view, it is morally dubious that any sum should be deducted from benefits set at subsistence level.

Parker (1992), discussing 'women, credit and debt' in society, argues:

'... There are those households which have chronically low incomes because they are dependent on state benefits ... For such households, the normal expectations of life as a twentieth century consumer *cannot be sustained other than by recourse to credit* or, *occasionally, a Social Fund loan from the DSS*' [My italics]

(p. 234).

Parker further shows that women are more likely to be involved in coping with debt and may also experience its effects more keenly than men (p. 234). The women are involved

'in a daily battle, not just to make money available for household durables but, more basically, to ensure that a roof is kept over the household's head, that fuel continues to be readily available and that adequate supplies of food are obtained'.

She concludes, with evidence, that 'at the lowest level of income, distinctions between budgeting, access to credit and becoming indebted are blurred' (p. 234).

What this means, of course, is that the struggle for survival is unending, time consuming and anxiety provoking. As Graham (1992) points out, whether one takes absolute or relative poverty as a yardstick, the effects on health are beyond doubt. 'Both concepts suggest that the struggle to make ends meet is fought out in and against the routines which sustain health' (p. 215). 'Food is the major item to be paid for within the family's residual income. It is also the item of expenditure over which a mother is most likely to exert control' (p. 219).

Graham describes the strategies which some mothers adopt – bones for soups, stewing meat for the children and gravy for themselves. However, this is not often the way of life adopted by neglectful parents, who may have had few experiences in childhood on which to model their culinary activities. Nor does contemporary society with its highly advertised, tempting and expensive convenience foods encourage such experiments with food. So the very real problems of managing on inadequate income for children's health are compounded by the limitations of the parents. I am confident that the physical health of the families, adults and children, about whom we are concerned, would, if rigorously assessed, reveal nutritional deficiencies affecting many aspects of functioning and energy levels which are needed to cope efficiently in difficult circumstances.

This book is focused on issues which directly affect the practice of those who work with neglectful families. It is clear that poverty is such an issue but it is one over which workers have very little control. To be impotent in the face of such deprivation and disadvantage is exceedingly stressful. It may increase reluctance to attribute 'blame' or responsibility to those attempting to cope with such adverse circumstances: what, then, is the role of workers and local agencies when the problem is treated elsewhere? First, there is, of course, corporate responsibility to address the deficiencies of provision for poor families, in or out of work. Second, workers with neglectful families will have a particularly important role to ensure that they have received their full entitlement.

Third, there will be occasions when additional financial help within the existing framework is necessary and helpful. However, the analysis of such help provided in cases of abusive (including neglectful) families shows that this often seems to do little to improve the situation. It therefore seems important regularly to review financial help offered in the context of an overall assessment of family functioning. Whatever the reality of the material needs there may be occasions when increased requests indicate a deteriorating situation or that a problem is not what it seems to be. The illustration, given earlier, of Paul's family (The

Bridge Consultancy 1995) selling furniture and equipment merits reflection. Experience has shown on the one hand that if it becomes known that financial help is available for some needs and not for others, the pragmatic claimant will adjust their claims accordingly (and who can blame them?). On the other hand, it is possible that lying behind such requests there may be needs of a more dangerous kind – for drugs or alcohol, for example. It is naive to split off financial help from other kinds of support in forming an overall strategy for the family in question.

Cash and care: the division of responsibility

Finally, a matter which cannot be explored here in the depth which it deserves is the relationship between 'cash or care' in our present provision. There is a long running unresolved debate, concerning the proper balance between provision based on general entitlement for a particular class of citizens and discretionary provision which caters for unique individual needs (Titmuss 1971; Stevenson 1970). Discretionary provision of the kind which is relevant to neglectful families is available nationally from the Social Fund but also from local authority social service departments under Section 17 of The Children Act 1989 (formerly Section 1 and Section 12 in Scotland). There has been extensive study of both powers (see for example Hill and Laing 1979; Huby & Dix 1992; Wilson 1993).

Neither is satisfactory in its present form. Within social security budgets, payments under the Social Fund and Section 17 are small but not negligible. In 1990/91, £223 million were dispersed from the Social Fund in grants or loans and its local variability and annual cycle have given rise to criticism. There have also always been dramatic variations between local authorities in the sums spent. Thus, for example, in 1987/88, three local authorities each spent nearly £1 000 000 and two only £4000 each, reflecting sharp differences in policy, as well as perceived need.

There has been, and will no doubt continue to be, intense resistance by local authorities to any extension of these financial duties and powers. Such resistance arises in part from moral objections to an increase in discretionary powers, in part from a (justified) fear that central government might impose more financial burdens on local government. However, the history of Section 1, now Section 17, grants is a depressing one. Lack of enthusiasm for the provisions has resulted in a kind of 'tactic of avoidance' so that, despite some research, their purpose, achievements and limitations have not been adequately evaluated by social service departments. Indeed, as poverty has become deeper and more widespread and local authorities more starved of resources, it is hardly surprising that there should be a conspiracy of silence. Nor does the evidence concerning the way financial help is presently dispersed by social workers give confidence that matters could be improved without a radical management initiative.

There remain, however, some searching questions concerning the most effective ways of using money to help neglectful families, and others whose material and environmental circumstances are particularly desperate at certain points in their lives. Field level workers need further guidance on the uses to which such funds might be put; there are wide variations between local authorities, some of which are a result of 'custom and practice' rather than a settled policy. Provided that it is used thoughtfully, the existence of limited discretionary financial powers is a useful ingredient in intervention. The present situation is a muddle.

Virtually all the neglectful families on whom we focus live on benefit or on extremely low incomes and many of them have severe problems in managing their money. Furthermore, the difficulties which are commonly experienced by families in chronic poverty are likely to be enhanced by the personal limitations of some of the parents in question, in particular when learning disabilities affect the capacity to budget or plan. As we shall discuss later, the relationships with the wider family and the local community may be deficient or tense, which lessens material and practical support available to tide families over at times of particular need. These are precisely the families who may not be able to 'pop next door or down to Mum's' to borrow some tea and sugar till the giro comes.

In this discussion I have stressed the unremitting strain and disadvantage which poverty on this scale creates for the adults and children in many families, including most of those whom we describe as neglectful and who may be less competent than others in battling with the difficulties. One hopes, and is entitled to assume, that this dimension is well appreciated by those who work with such families. The challenge is to incorporate that dimension of understanding as part of an active plan for support and intervention; hitherto, action in poverty has too often been reactive, for example, the 'Friday afternoon, no giro' phenomenon, without a sense of continuity and purpose.

However, it is unfair to place the responsibility for this on field workers. For social workers in social service departments, organisational ambivalence about its discretionary powers has given them little training or policy guidance about their constructive use. For both social workers and health visitors (and perhaps other professionals) the complex causes and effects of poverty, debt and mismanagement in neglectful families have been given insufficient emphasis in training and staff development so that there is sometimes a naive reliance on material help to alleviate much more deep-seated difficulties.

The tasks for those involved at field level are therefore:

- To know the details of *this* family's financial position, including debt and deductions from benefit and to ensure full entitlement is secured.
- To seek to understand and to feel the impact of poverty on individual members of *this* family – which deficits are felt most keenly by children and adults.
- To consider the particular difficulties in managing which *this* family experiences.
- In the light of the above, to identify and integrate financial advice or assistance into a protection plan.

However, even in such inhospitable financial times, the responsibility for the alleviation of poverty obviously goes beyond the workers at field level. Leaving aside wider questions of the adequacy of benefit levels, the problems of deductions of social fund grants and loans, and (closely connected) of the local authority's exercise of its discretionary powers all need to be considered urgently. They have a particular relevance to the families with whom we are concerned.

Chapter 4
Neglectful Families: The Wider Context

As Fig. 2.1 indicates, there is a constant dynamic interplay between, on the one hand, the family and the individuals which comprise it and, on the other, the various systems and groups of people outside it. This chapter seeks to understand those families in which children are neglected, with reference to informal systems – the wider family, the neighbourhood and cultural influences. There is a substantial research literature, much of it from the USA, which demonstrates that families in which children are seriously neglected are, in comparison with other families, very socially isolated (Polansky *et al.* 1985(a); Polansky *et al.* 1985(b)). Polansky argues that this social isolation is found in families of abused children generally. However, this is challenged by Seagull (1987), who claims that the research evidence for this is much stronger in the case of neglect than in other kinds of abuse. She also points to the associated finding that many neglectful families bring this isolation upon themselves. Gaudin (1993), summarising the findings for the US Department of Health and Human Services, concludes: 'Neglectful parents typically lack strong informal helpful resources' (p. 18). This is the observation of many practitioners in this country and is confirmed by such research in the UK as that of Creighton (1986). She examined the information on children registered for neglect in the two previous years and found that social isolation was the second highest of 37 factors which workers were asked to rank in order of their severity of effect.

Before further discussing the evidence of social isolation, however, we need to remind ourselves that the phrase 'social isolation' carries within it a value judgement. Isolation is deemed to be undesirable and suggests that there is a deficit which must be made good. Whilst this will be a reasonable goal in many aspects and domains of the lives of parents and children, when it is applied indiscriminately it may distract attention from the negative or damaging effects of some kinds of interaction. This is particularly salient in relation to the wider family to which we now turn.

The wider family

Whether one is examining the nuclear or the wider family, an analysis of power and influence is inevitable. In the families we are here considering, it is too easy to move from the observation that they are often isolated in certain ways from their relatives to the assumption that it would be good to lessen the isolation. But that is naive, unless we take into account that in the course of seeking to improve the quality of these interactions, we may bring to the surface negative as well as positive emotions or may seem to reinforce power in certain members through legitimising their intervention. There is a particular danger, a false logic, in moving from the finding that neglectful families are 'in deficit' socially to an assumption that more 'input' from existing sources is needed to make good the deficit. As Gaudin (1993) points out: 'The social networks of neglectful mothers appear to be dominated by relatives who are critical rather than supportive. Interactions with relatives may be frequent but not very helpful' (p. 18). As Seagull (1987) tersely puts it: 'Considering the very negative rearing of the majority of abusive parents, staying away from their parents could be indicative of good judgement' (p. 49).

It is surprising how little attempt there has been in the study of families and children to disentangle the complex issues surrounding the notion of 'support' by a network of relatives from other kinds of social support. There has been much more work in the field of adult community care, some of which (for example Finch (1989) which explores 'obligations' of family members to each other) would repay application to other areas of family life. The so called 'nuclear' families which are the focus of our concern are often lone mothers with unstable partnerships. I know of no systematic study in this country concerning the quality of relationships between such mothers and their relatives.

In the USA, Coohey (1995) examined the significance of mutual aid between neglectful mothers and their mothers. She comments that 'despite the burgeoning literature, no study in the child maltreatment area has focused on the exchange relations between abusive mothers and their mothers' (p. 886).

In a carefully constructed, multi cultural study she reached the following interesting conclusions, from the accounts of the neglectful mothers themselves:

'Mothers of neglectful mothers when compared with others, are either less willing or less able to give emotional support to their neglectful daughters and neglectful daughters are less interested in receiving emotional support'

(p.893).

Coohey acknowledges that, from these findings, we cannot conclude the extent to which the present reflects past patterns: whether the older woman's inability to give to her daughter as a child is carried through to adult life. However it seems probable. In general, neglectful daughters said they received 'significantly less emotional and instrumental support from their mothers' (p. 893). (There was, however, a very significant unexplained exception of potential importance: very little difference between the sample and control group on help with baby sitting.) The general findings should not be viewed too pessimistically. The amount of help and mutual support offered in these exchanges was still significant, even if less than in the control group. For example, 41% of these 'neglectful' mothers described their mothers as 'really listening/providing companionship'; 49% gave money or loans.

The above describes only one, small scale study, from another country, of one dimension, adult mother–daughter relationships which affect the well-being of families. It is cited here to bring to the fore the need for sensitivity to, and detailed appreciation of, the significance of such family relationships. Neither of these general propositions, that support of the wider family is valuable and the specific observation that abusive and neglectful parents frequently lack such support, is controversial amongst professionals. It will be 'nodded through' at conferences. Yet there seems to be a dysfunction between this acceptance and a real understanding of its particular significance. Indeed, 'family, friends and neighbours' are often lumped together in discussion. Yet, when neglectful families are isolated from their wider network of relatives, the implications are particularly grave. They are cut off from a source of support and help which is of immense significance to most families (McGlone *et al.* 1996). This help may be 'instrumental' or 'affective' (Polansky 1985b). In well functioning families these are often inseparable and interact to positive effect. The type of instrumental help which is commonest is of two kinds. There are small scale financial transactions; loans and gifts, or gifts in kind, may offer a day by day life line to those in poverty. Indeed, they may reduce dependence on debt from exploitative lenders. Second, sharing in the care of children in diverse ways relieves stress and opens up employment opportunities. Both these forms of support are affected by the position and age of the older generation. The younger the mothers, the more likely it is that the older generation will still be caught up in their own child rearing and employment and have less to offer to their adult children and grandchildren.

'Affective' help is less tangible but profoundly important; the offering of advice and sympathy, the taken-for-granted currency of everyday interaction, may have particularly positive effects when offered within close emotional relationships. These relationships are not all mediated via the adults to the children; not infrequently, the children, individually, relate to particular relatives who may offer them a supplement to or different dimension from, life at home. The ordinary price that is paid for such support is exposure to a certain amount of tension, conflict, hurt and anger. But, as Seagull (1987) suggests, that price may be too high for some neglectful parents who have learned not to get too psychologically close to others, for fear of being emotionally hurt (p. 48).

There is now accumulated evidence from a range of UK literature that, whatever lip service is paid to the notion of support from the wider family, its implications have not been incorporated into child protection work. For example, the comprehensive assessment guide (Department of Health 1988, the 'orange book') devotes very little attention to the wider family. Despite the use of genograms and eco-maps (pp. 81–5) there is nothing in the guide to suggest the particular significance of these relationships, which places them in a different order of significance from many others loosely described as in 'the community'. Another example of 'missed opportunities' lies in the many child abuse inquiries which have been the subject of detailed scrutiny and discussion since 1974. In a number of these, relatives (often grandparents) have featured as expressing concern and anxiety about the children (see, for example, White, Leanne 1994). It has been apparent that social workers were uncomfortable, even ambivalent about the role of such people. Yet few commentators have gone further than to criticise the failure of workers to take seriously the warnings of relatives – often linked in reports to references to neighbours by placing them in the same category. The study of inquiry reports (Department of Health 1991) pays scant attention (pp. 81–2) to the deeper aspects of relatives' involvement – presumably reflecting the reports themselves. Most of them considered the issue solely in terms of risk assessment and it is apparent that workers had received little guidance and help in appraising the significance of the tangled and turbulent relationships which so often existed in the wider families of those with whom they worked. This is often very problematic, raising questions not only of relatives' motives for referral and apparent concern, but of standards and criteria by which to judge the situation.

The importance of this missing dimension has been stressed in the 'messages from research' (Department of Health 1988) in which a 'myopia' about the child's family is the subject of comment. 'The common preoccupation was with the nuclear aspect... The significance of wider patterns of kinship and other sources of emotional support was often overlooked, (p. 49). (Note 'emotional' support only is commented upon.) This comment is in part derived from Farmer and Owen (1995), whose perceptive comments take us further in understanding the significance of this subject. They point out that, in investigating child abuse and neglect, workers often did not clarify relationships with the wider family even in 'stock taking' occasions such as the case conference: 'The lack of family support or social isolation was not always known. Even when it had been discussed, *it was often treated as a matter for counselling* [my italics]' (p. 285).

This, of course, is the nub of the matter. As we have shown, the extent and nature of wider family supports, their strengths and deficiencies, are important in the here and now, in making assessments and purposeful plans for the present situation. It is not simply a 'matter for counselling'. It is also important in understanding more of what Farmer and Owen describe as the 'aetiology' of the abuse or neglect, or 'the germ of an explanatory theory'. This explanatory theory is not simply of historical interest – how did these parents come to be as they are – but also of immediate relevance to the present family situation. As we shall discuss later, it is imperative to search for the meaning of parental 'omissions' – what is it that they cannot do for their children and why? How far is this related to the care which they in turn were not given? What, therefore, should professionals be trying to achieve in relation to these wider family relationships? Farmer and Owen point out that 'information was presented in a disconnected way or linked simply to the diagnosis or risk'. Therefore, its 'implication for planning often went unrecognised' (pp. 136–7).

That these deficiencies in the approach to work with families have been acknowledged in the influential research discussed above gives cause for some optimism, as does the present enthusiastic and receptive professional audience for the notion of 'family group conferences' which originated in New Zealand. These developments are described at length in a parallel book in this series (Marsh & Crow 1997). The process itself of mobilising relatives to discuss and plan for children in difficulty, will not be discussed here. Rather, it is used as an illustration of the underlying importance of the general approach to the involvement of family members. As Marsh and Crow point out, the evidence of the importance of the family network for nearly all families is powerful and 'pivotal in child welfare'. Furthermore, 'diversity is the hallmark of the modern family, with values, employment patterns, culture, race and many other factors interacting and resulting in a unique blend for each family' (p. 28). To start with, as they succinctly put it: 'to work with the family, we have to ask the family who the family is' (p. 30). They view the wider family as a 'psycho-social entity' in which different members, over time, exert more or less influence. They discuss the meaning and impact which the wider family group has on its sub system, in particular, the part it plays in the development of a child's identity.

The fact that this approach has been pinned to a particular innovation, that of family group conferences, has at once both positive and negative elements. It is positive because the idea is concrete, innovative and challenging. These conferences have caught the imagination of a group of practitioners and what is learnt from this particular way of working can surely be applied more generally. It is potentially negative if they prove to be a passing phase of interest, almost a 'gimmick' which loses its attractions as the inevitable difficulties become apparent. That is to say, if the essence of an important idea is lost in reservations about the practical operations of a particular event.

There is one way, however, in which this trend may be seen to be part of a more substantial development and, thus, likely to have a more permanent impact on child welfare work. The movement towards greater inclusion and involvement of family members in the lives of particular families is associated with earlier work towards 'partnership' with parents, which has been extensively researched and discussed in recent research (see for example, Thoburn *et al.* 1995). It is part of an ethos in which power should be more effectively and sincerely shared by professionals with those we describe as 'informal carers', who usually play the most critical part in the lives of the children upon whom our concern is focused. However, as with the concepts of 'partnership with parents', there has to be a determined effort neither to idealise nor to minimise the capacity of relatives to meet the deficits for children so often found in neglectful families. The way to avoid either extreme has to be by systematic exploration of these unique interactions. One is tempted to say that the precise nature of the explanatory theory is much less important than the underlying drive on the part of the workers to make some sense of the relationships between family members to find some coherent patterns between family needs and deficits, to ask what has been on offer in the past and what might be offered in the future. The worker's image of the family needs to be expanded, so that the potential and limitations of the wider family network in relation to the needs of the nuclear family are better understood.

Ethnic and cultural factors

There are serious difficulties in relating the topic of this book, neglect, to ethnic and cultural factors in ways which will be helpful to practitioners. Some problems arise from the lack of research and knowledge in the UK in this area. There are three dimensions to this: first, we need much more detailed information about the child rearing practices of particular groups. These are subtle processes which cannot be viewed through a telescope. Second, we need to know what lessons, difficulties or changes of behaviour arise from living as a minority group within a majority culture. Third, the above has to be applied to the problem of neglect. However, as we shall see, this relative dearth of knowledge is itself significant because of the anxiety and sensitivity surrounding the investigation of culture. Nonetheless, in my view, the time is overdue for an attempt to discuss these extremely important issues.

The term 'culture' is used here to mean patterns of shared experience and behaviour through which personal identity and social structures are developed. Culture is, thus, a concept which extends beyond race and ethnicity and, in our context, has particular salience in terms of social class as well as ethnic difference. However, we do well also to remind ourselves that ethnicity does not only mean 'non white'. Rather, it refers to the distinctive identity of particular groups, derived in part from racial, religious and cultural affiliations. It is important, also, to recognise that racial, ethnic and even class origins are not, of themselves, sufficient to explain variations in child rearing. Culture is located within prevailing norms and values in which there are contradictions and tensions and in which present norms and values may clash with those passed on from families of origin. This observation is of particular importance in some work with ethnic minorities where, for example, there is sharp tension between parents and teenage girls, although care must be taken not to exaggerate the racial significance of behaviour common to many families of all ethnic groups who have adolescent children.

References to child maltreatment occur throughout history and across cultures. However, since the 1960s, influenced by the focus on the subject in the USA, there has been a burgeoning literature (Korbin 1991). It has demonstrated wide variations in definition, often bound up with the prevailing economic and social conditions of the time, as well as underlying value systems (Korbin 1991). There is now general understanding that child abuse is a socially constructed concept and hence susceptible to different interpretation in time and place. Korbin argues that this 'presents a dilemma'. 'Failure to allow for a cultural perspective promotes an ethnocentric position in which one's own cultural beliefs and practices are presumed to be preferable and superior to all others.' Yet, 'a stance of extreme cultural relativism in which all judgements of humane treatment of children are suspended in the name of cultural rights, may be used to justify a lesser standard of care for some children' (p. 68). Maitra (1995) argues that culture must be examined but as part of

> 'an examination of the interactive effects of racism, minority status and socio economic disadvantage with each group's cultural systems. A focus on racial discrimination alone runs the risk of conferring the minority person within two stereotypes – of victim, or its mirror image, the rigidly idealised "black" identity.'
>
> (p. 156)

Korbin (1991) suggests that we need a coherent framework in which to place this debate. She suggests that there are three levels: first, differences between cultures; second, individual departures from acceptable behaviour within cultures and third, harm to children occasioned by social and economic conditions outside the family's control (p. 68).

The third of these has already been discussed in the context of increased poverty and associated disadvantage within the UK in recent years. As has often been pointed out, families from some ethnic minorities are disproportionately represented in this disadvantage (Channer & Parton 1990; Dutt & Phillips 1996). However, vitally important as it is, this is not the point at issue here in which we seek to explore the implications of cultural difference on the problem of neglect. Korbin's first two categories go to the heart of the British practitioner's dilemma: what are genuinely distinctive cultural practices and what are deviations from the 'internal' cultural norms of a particular group?

The now extensive British literature in child abuse and neglect generally has not much advanced our understanding of cultural factors within the UK in relation to the problem of neglect, or indeed, of other forms of abuse. In the face of widespread racism, explicit or implicit, including a tendency amongst professionals to 'pathologise' cultural variations, many social workers have thought it preferable to draw attention to the racism which causes suffering to children and families and to expose racist assumptions by professionals rather than to dwell on variations and subtleties of child rearing practices. This is strongly argued, as in Dutt and Phillips (1996). Yet, failure to recognise the significance of culture is in the end a kind of racism. It can result in a kind of professional immobilisation, in which difference may be ignored, or wrongly attributed to cultural difference rather than to the problems of certain individuals. Underlying this, there is confusion concerning the implications of 'cultural relativism', an inability to sort out what differences in child rearing practices can be acceptable in the context of contemporary society and what cannot be accepted. Channer and Parton (1990) refer to 'reconstructed racism which leads to a failure to act at all' (p. 112).

This is a difficult and delicate matter but one has only to look at the realities of the dilemmas which child welfare practitioners face in day to day work to see that it has to be faced. Some agonising problems centre on issues, such as female genital circumcision, outside the scope of this book. But to focus only on such extreme matters distorts the debate. The only honest way to work is to approach families of different origins respectfully, in the expectation that there are likely to be variations in child rearing and with the curiosity to find out about those which are relevant to the circumstances of the case. This does not absolve the worker from making a judgement, in certain matters, as to whether the care offered is 'good enough' by the standards and knowledge of our time. This is the best we can do. It should ensure that we do not fall into either extreme: of cultural dogmatism – 'ours is the best way' – or cultural relativism – 'anything goes'.

A measure of curiosity (some would call it 'nosiness'!) provided it is focused, is a prerequisite for good professional practice. There has been a puzzling lack of curiosity about this most interesting and important dimension of work with families and children. It is probably best explained in terms of anxiety and fear either of being racist or of being perceived as such. Channer and Parton (1990) argue that 'culturally relative practice must be abandoned since it leads to simplistic, polarised and stereotypical views of clients and their situations and does nothing to challenge workers' own norms and values' (p. 117).

When we come to neglect, there has been virtually no exploration of the application of the concept, its definitions and examples, to different ethnic and cultural groups in the UK. There is no evidence – and one would not expect there to be – that serious neglect, as the term is generally used in this country, is more common amongst one group than another. There are not likely to be major differences between cultural groups in the basic physical care of infants and very young children who are being brought up in the social and environmental context of this country.

Although fascinating, it is probably misleading to place much emphasis on unfamiliar practice from far off countries. However, some illustrations are of value in raising our sensitivity to the differences in child rearing which might have to be taken into account within the British context. Rashid (1996), for example, examines culture in relation to the theory of attachment. He argues that 'attachment, like bereavement, is shaped or patterned by the culture in which it takes place' (p. 61). He points out that child care professionals might 'attempt to evaluate the strength and nature of the attachment relationship ... by using culturally, specific notions like direct eye contact' (p. 61). He gives examples of cultures in which gaze is associated with disrespect and discouraged by mothers. In the Gusii (Kenya), it is suggested that child rearing practices are designed to lower competitiveness in mothers and children. This may lead children to appear understimulated and more passive.

Thus, one of the accepted indicators of neglect – lack of stimulation – is another possible area of difficulty; how much stimulation, of what kind and at what ages is it usually given in the minority groups represented in this country? This would merit further study.

More obviously bound to culture and experience are various practices involving health. Whilst there is the same goal, there may be deeply held differences of the means to that end. Korbin (1991) gives an example of Turkish mothers' belief that a child of 18 months must be kept very warm indeed by Western standards (p. 69).

A study by Hackett and Hackett (1994) is particularly valuable because it investigated child rearing practices in relation to Gujarati and white British children brought up in the UK. It reminds us of differences of emphasis in upbringing which can reasonably be seen as differing routes to the same goal, that of rearing healthy, well socialised children. It is interesting that, although closely linked, the differences relate more to other issues of abuse (physical and emotional) than to neglect. For example, British parents believed that smacking was more necessary than Gujarati parents but, in fact, there were few differences between them in reported frequency. Gujarati parents were much less likely to tolerate 'mess' (water, paint, etc.) than British parents, more punitive about toilet training and bed wetting but much more relaxed about bedtimes and sleeping arrangements. Most important, the emotional, 'Gujarati preference methods of discipline' (p. 198) (withdrawing love, bringing in an authority figure, etc.) were clear; British parents tended to disapprove of these methods. The Gujarati children were found to be better adjusted, despite the fact that some of their child rearing practices were, by conventional Western standards, less acceptable. Even that finding, however, reminds us that 'adjustment' is itself a culturally contested concept. What is a *good child*? None of the examples of difference chosen by the authors brought issues of neglect, that is, omission of care, to the fore. Rather, they challenged some of the cultural assumptions about 'best ways' of disciplining and bringing up children. However, the cultural differences are within relatively narrow parameters of 'ordinary' upbringing – a far cry from seriously neglectful families.

The above examples are intended to shed light on the fascinating and diverse patterns of child rearing which one is sure to find when cultural norms are explored. Such explorations challenge us at a deep level: in terms of our preconceptions, of our ability to learn from others and our ability to sort out whether what we observe is just different, or *worryingly* different. If it is the latter, is it worrying because we believe there is an important clash of cultures or is it because the situation is unacceptable to both cultures? It is thus both emotionally and intellectually demanding and requires a professional person to be as well informed as possible. The present deficiencies in knowledge and research on the subject of 'culture and neglect' make it all the more important to reach into the cultural groups with whom we are working, to utilise fully the knowledge which reposes within those communities. This will help workers to weigh up the significance of what they see, which is especially important when there are a number of possible indicators of neglect under consideration. It is about a holistic picture, in which (with some exceptions) a particular child rearing practice is not in itself a determinant of neglect. It is self evident that professionals of the same cultural groups are invaluable. But their absence does not excuse lack of curiosity on the part of the others; nor should particular individuals representing particular ethnic groups have to bear too heavy a burden of 'understanding'. Furthermore, the availability of such individuals is of greatest value in raising awareness of and respect for cultural values amongst their colleagues, not to 'ghettoise' services to ethnic minorities (Owusa-Bempah 1998).

There is a further dimension of this issue to which Korbin (1991) draws attention: that is, the possibility that there are particular categories of children who may be more susceptible to maltreatment, including, abuse, than others. This is a highly sensitive matter and one should note that Korbin's analysis relates to cross cultural differences between countries or continents and does not necessarily take into account the effects of prevailing values on minorities in this country. Part of Korbin's analysis relates to the care of children who may be less valued than others, by reason of their family status (e.g. stepchildren), gender or disability. It is commonly known, for example, that in some countries boys receive preferential treatment, including basic care in infancy. (This preference was also deeply imbedded in British culture in terms, for example, of education and inheritance rights.) Attitudes to children with learning or physical disabilities may be of shame and rejection; this may be difficult to observe since, in some cultures, children may be hidden from view (literally or symbolically). But, if they are rejected, neglect may be more serious and cannot be tolerated within our society. Thus, when children are culturally devalued, serious moral issues are posed for the workers. For the rest, Korbin points out that, across all cultures particular children in a family may be scapegoated. The reasons given may differ but they are often associated with circumstances of birth.

In addition to raised awareness of cultural variations in child rearing itself, there are important matters concerning the impact on families of the investigative and interventive processes which arise in cases of abuse and neglect. Owusa-Bempah (forthcoming 1998), in an interesting study, has explored the application of principles of confidentiality in social work across cultures, using African culture as an example. He points out that, in British society, confidentiality assumes an 'individual–community dichotomy' whereas in African cultures the individual derives his or her sense of identity from belonging to a family, group or community (p. 1). However, this may mean that the notion of confidentiality is significant to the family group as a whole and does not necessarily imply a willingness to share information with 'outsiders' such as the professionals. It may, however, have positive implications for the arrangements of 'family group conferences' in certain circumstances (Marsh & Crow 1997). 'Family secrets' may be shared much more widely than in some British families.

Sharing family knowledge with the professionals has been noted as problematic by others; as Channer and Parton (1990) remark 'the reporting of such incidents may be perceived as betrayal of or disloyalty to the whole community' (p. 119). There may also be powerful feelings of shame and stigma which inhibit communication with the official world. When one adds to this the experiences of racism which such families may have had, there are formidable difficulties in establishing trusting and effective relationships. However, this all needs to be put in the general context of contemporary British social welfare. Ethnic minorities may be no more distrustful of professionals than white working class people who are gravely disadvantaged and marginalised; social workers, in particular, may be perceived as dangerous.

The above illustrations of sensitive cultural issues, concerning confidentiality, shame or stigma, are simply indications of bridges which have to be built in effective work. They are quite inadequate and superficial in relation to the diverse groups, both recently settled and long established, that form our contemporary society. Even were more detailed research available, there can be no substitute for the willingness to listen and learn on the part of individual workers. Maitra (1995), for example, gives an interesting example of assumptions one cannot take for granted in working between cultures. One such is 'that cultural rules may not be broken ... it requires great patience, ingenuity and consultation with bicultural colleagues to discover culturally sanctioned "get out" clauses' (p. 163).

This chapter began with a consideration of the relationships which exist between the members of the wider family network and pointed out that there is evidence that these are frequently damaging and unsatisfactory in the lives of families of neglectful children, resulting in considerable social isolation. It went on to consider the significance of cultural factors, especially in relation to ethnic minorities, when working with neglectful families. However, in separating these two themes, there is a danger of splitting off discussion of cultural factors from the people who mediate them. As children, the adults around us are the purveyors of culture. Therefore, how we feel about them affects the way cultural values are internalised, absorbed, distorted, resisted or rejected.

The local community

We turn now to consider the local community, whose norms may or may not be congruent with those of particular families but which will play a crucial part in day to day life. There has been little professional discussion in the UK concerning the position of abusive and neglectful families within their local community. Yet discussion with practitioners quickly reveals a keen awareness of the sense of social isolation which both adults and children experience. Workers will need no convincing that it is a dominant and distressing aspect of the daily lives of some neglected children, whose physical appearance, poor clothing and personal hygiene quickly make them outcasts in the school. Children's wish for acceptance amongst their peers, based on a strong sense of conformity, makes the situation of neglected children at school particularly painful to observe.

This general view that social isolation is a significant factor in such cases is borne out by a considerable body of research from the USA, often as part of what is described as an 'ecological' approach to the understanding of family problems. Polansky and his colleagues have devoted particular attention to the isolation of neglectful mothers, not only in relation to their wider families but within their local communities. They studied such women (1985(a); 1985(b)) in two projects, rural and urban, in which neglectful mothers and a control group were interviewed as to their perceptions of neighbours' helpfulness. The striking differences between the two groups is illustrated in Table 4.1.

Table 4.1 A study on perceptions of helpfulness: proportions of women who say three or more neighbours will help them.

Service		Neglect (%)	Control (%)
1	Lend five dollars	22.4	55.0
2	Lend food, clothing	23.7	45.0
3	Comfort when feeling low	25.0	56.3
4	Prepare food when sick, absent	26.3	51.3
5	Give ride to store, doctor	30.3	45.0
6	Rescue if in police trouble	19.7	45.0
7	Listen to problems with sympathy	26.3	56.3
8	Babysit for children free	21.9	33.9

From Polansky *et al.* 1985a.

The conclusions reported in the rural study are particularly valuable. First, the hypothesis that neglectful behaviour reflected the community mores was not supported (p. 46). Part of the problem, indeed, is the very fact that such families stand out from their neighbours. Second, the mothers perceived themselves to be less integrated in informal helping networks than other rural women, and more lonely. Children also were less involved in school than other poor children. Third, and importantly, the geographical areas studied were not found to be generally unsupportive. Rather the neglectful families were perceived by others to be 'more in need of help' and less likely to be asked for help themselves.

'Since reciprocating favours plays so large a role in most networks, neglectful families were typically in an unfortunate position. Their feelings of aloneness, then, are not just subjective for they are apt to be viewed as deviant and to be distanced by others.'

(Polansky 1985a, p. 47)

Polansky *et al.* (1985(b)), in discussing both the rural and urban studies, confirmed and extended the rural findings in that 'according to the characteristics of and judgements by their neighbours', these women 'were no worse off than others who were offering adequate child care'. But the neglectful mothers themselves painted a different picture. On average, they viewed their locales as less friendly and less helpful. These findings were confirmed by a later study (Gaudin & Polansky 1986) which elicited the views of 'ordinary' people about neglectful families, to establish 'social distance'. The researchers asked a number of questions, which were indicators of social distance, concerning the willingness of people to engage with such families, in varying degrees of proximity. (Vignettes were used to standardise responses.) Thus, for example, respondents were asked whether they would: say 'hello' to a certain family; let their child eat at the family's house; have a child from that family over for a meal, etc. The findings have three points of particular interest. First, there was some reluctance to associate with such families; second, it grew stronger as the degree of 'closeness' or proximity increased; third, the respondents attributed much greater reluctance 'to the community' than to themselves as individuals. It is probable that this indicates that respondents felt guilty about their own feelings and found it easier to project negative feelings into the vaguer, more impersonal, 'community'. Gaudin and Polansky discussed the positive and negative implications of this finding. For example, they pointed out that, despite the reluctance, 90% of the respondents said they as individuals were willing to speak and offer help to typical neglectful parents. On the other hand, respondents suggested that the great majority (67%) of their neighbours '(i.e. the community) would speak with a neglectful parent only when necessary and only 40% would be willing to babysit for the family' (pp. 10-11). The ambivalence is striking.

Such findings take us back to the question of the extent to which, in crude terms, the families may be said to bring their isolation on themselves by behaviour which alienates them from others. Our model for understanding the situation of such families helps us to see that this is a vicious circle in which certain behaviours lead to ostracism, which may in turn lead to anxiety and anger towards, or withdrawal from, the host community. In recent years, in the UK, the unattractive dynamics in this process have been exemplified in the colloquial phrase 'neighbours from hell' and by highly coloured accounts in the media of the hostility engendered between neighbours. There is no doubt that amongst such families there will be some who would be characterised as neglectful of their children. The observations made long ago by sociologists that the 'respectable' poor struggled to distance themselves from those who threatened that respectability stands the test of time well. In the community tensions so often apparent with neglectful families, we see these dynamics in operation and the fear of 'stigma by association' (Stevenson 1970). It seems likely that the situation is made worse by the fact that some of the housing estates in which such families live have as a whole become 'ghettoised' by the failure of government to see the dangers of the policies, or lack of them, in creating such concentrations of disadvantaged people. The struggle to stay 'respectable' has become even more intense in post Thatcher Britain, with the inevitable consequence of increased hostility to those who, by their image and behaviour, further damage the reputation of the estates.

Conclusions

In summary, then, the objectives of this chapter have been to examine the impact of the wider family, of the cultural and ethnic factors and of the local community on a neglectful family. An important part of our understanding is that these factors are not simply 'external' to the nuclear family. They are part of it, penetrating the feelings and attitudes of the individuals, in terms of both past and present dynamics. Whilst there are huge gaps in our knowledge and understanding, such an approach leads to a more sophisticated awareness of the complex dynamics underlying these interactions and should help us develop strategies for action, some of which are discussed later.

This is not quite as daunting as it sounds when it is applied to particular families in particular situations. It leads us to ask:

- Who are the key people outside the nuclear family for the individuals within it?
- Do they help or hinder 'good enough' parenting? In what ways?
- Are they amenable to change, if necessary? If so, how?
- How might we fill some of the 'people' gaps in the lives of parents and children?
- What cultural factors, especially in relation to ethnic minorities, might be relevant to the assessment of neglect? How do we seek to find out their significance and weigh up their importance?

Chapter 5

The Parents

Issues affecting understanding

There is evidence from the recent research funded by the Department of Health, both within the Studies in Child Protection (Birchall & Hallett 1995; Farmer & Owen 1995; Hallett 1995; Thoburn *et al.* 1995) and outside it (Wilding & Thoburn 1997) that neglect features very prominently in child abuse referrals in the UK either by itself or associated with other forms of maltreatment, notably physical abuse. In Wilding and Thoburn's study covering three social service departments, out of 349 child protection referrals of children under 8 years, 64% were for neglect and some of the 23% for physical abuse included neglect (Fig. 5.1).

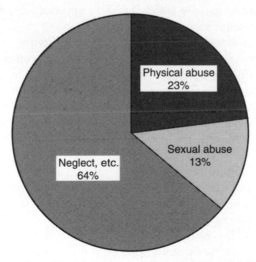

Fig. 5.1 Reasons for referral (child protection referrals only) (Wilding & Thoburn 1997). *Notes: n* = 349. Sexual abuse refers to referral concerning sexual abuse, including three cases combined with concerns about physical abuse. Physical abuse refers to referrals concerning physical abuse on its own, and those combined with concerns about other types of maltreatment. Neglect refers to all other child protection referrals with no concerns stated about either physical or sexual abuse.

Wilding and Thoburn (Table 6, p. 9) also present some figures concerning the types of maltreatment within the broad headings. Of the 116 interviewed from the total sample, 59% were in the category of physical neglect, of which 34% were classified as inadequate supervision; 23% were emotionally neglected which included extreme spouse abuse (17%).

A number of such referrals reveal 'incidents' of omission of care rather than persisting problems. Such cases have implications for preventative services. They are not, however, the main focus of this book, which is upon families in which neglect may be described as 'intermittent' or 'chronic'.

In the former case of 'intermittent neglect', parents are capable in general of providing adequate care but this is interrupted by sporadic breakdowns, often related to alcohol or drug misuse, during which children are placed at risk. In the latter cases, there is a persisting deficit in the care offered. Deficiencies in hygiene and nutrition may be evident but lack of parental supervision or stimulation may also be important or it may exist by itself. (Too great a concentration on the material environment has been known to lull workers into a false sense of security.)

What, then, can we say about the parents and these neglected children? The literature on neglect and associated problems of child maltreatment in recent years has been in some ways frustrating. Much of the American research clarifies and measures; an obsession with rating scales seems to drive some of it. This approach has much to offer in terms of greater precision in assessment, especially in cases of neglect. But it has two serious limitations so far as its utility for practitioners is concerned. First, the range of issues involved in neglectful families is so great that use of rating scales in general assessment is quite impracticable for field workers, such as social workers or health visitors, in the course of their ordinary work. However, a specific rating scale may be usefully employed for an element in assessment, especially when a particular issue relating to a member of the family has been identified as of concern.

The second limitation is more general and more contentious. The administration of such tests does not fit comfortably with the warm, co-operative relationships which many workers seek to establish with such families. Workers may feel that such tests do not 'get inside the people'. Certainly, they can only constitute an aid to judgement, either on occasion by direct use or as assistance 'in the background' to workers who must clarify the issues which worry them. As will be evident in this chapter, however, practitioners can benefit greatly from the knowledge which is acquired through the use of these techniques in research, provided they are subjected to rigorous analysis, for example, in relation to cultural bias, and are seen as an element in making judgements which are derived from different ways of understanding.

Much British research, led (and funded) by government priorities, has also been predominantly quantitative in its methodology, although liberally laced with case illustrations. The main focus of this extensive research has been on the processes of the formal child protection system and its effects on users, which is understandable in the context of its commissioning. It has provided in admirable detail information on general trends which can be used by officials and senior managers. But practitioners are left looking through a telescope when they need a microscope.

Thus, somehow, both the American and British literature on this subject leaves us somewhat distanced from the objects of our concern. This research emphasis has been paralleled in practice. Thoburn *et al.* (1996) comment:

> 'Whilst most analysts of child protection, policies and practice note the importance of considering such variables as the age of the child, the type of maltreatment and the identity of the person allegedly responsible, less attention has been paid to the many dimensions and biographies of those involved as individuals and families rather than abusing families or abused children... Professionals so often appeared to become mesmerised by abusive acts or symptoms of neglect or maltreatment and failed to understand the complex nature of the events and interactions leading to it.'

> (pp. 333–4)

Howe (1996) analyses this in depth in his detailed exploration of the reasons for what he describes as 'the analytically more shallow and increasingly performance orientated context of social theories and practices' (p. 77).

The extent of this shift of emphasis is powerfully illustrated by turning back to Mattinson and Sinclair's (1979) remarkable book *Mate and Stalemate*. The fieldwork for this took place in London local authorities at the time of the Maria Colwell inquiry (in 1973, see DHSS 1974), the impact of which was keenly felt. The year of its publication saw the election of the Conservative government and the beginning of what must surely now be seen as a massive onslaught on the values and the competence of the social work profession. The focus and style of *Mate and Stalemate*, which explored marital work with highly disturbed and disorganised families, using four different kinds of theory with psychodynamic origins, would make its publication today highly unlikely. Yet its general approach (not necessarily accepted uncritically) is precisely what is needed to put living flesh on the dry bones of so much contemporary research.

Politically driven priorities are part of the explanation for this practice vacuum but there are other, deeper factors as well. One reason for what may be described as 'losing the people' in research and practice discussion arises from the retreat from the use of theory which was perceived as potentially 'blaming' the people concerned, discussed earlier (Chapter 1). This is particularly relevant to neglect. The post war history of concern about neglect is instructive. In the 1950s and 1960s the term 'problem family' was commonly used to describe cases which troubled social workers and bore much resemblance to the families we are here considering (Philp 1963). The term became unacceptable, as awareness of post war problems of poverty and its attendant stresses was reawakened and the sociological critique of social workers as 'agents of social control' mounted.

As we commented in Chapter 1, the extent and nature of the external difficulties with which poor parents grappled led to a kind of revulsion against 'the diagnosis' of their troubles in terms of their own emotional or psychological difficulties, which seemed to carry with it implications of criticism or censure. In particular, there was a sharp reaction against classification or generalisation drawn from psychiatric or psycho-analytic sources. In more recent years, the growing concern and anger amongst professionals about poverty and disadvantage, of the growth of an 'underclass' (a word which itself engenders ambivalence), have strengthened resistance to any analysis of a family's predicament in which external factors are not stressed. The model of understanding presented here and the discussion of poverty and isolation will, I hope, reassure the reader that due weight is given to external stressors. The 'ecological' perspective is in itself an attempt to integrate various theories. Whatever the academic tensions between what might loosely be called a 'sociological' or 'psychological' view of such parents' difficulties, however uncertain workers may be about using terms or descriptions which might further stigmatise families, the fact remains that when such workers come together, they recognise something that is distinctive about the difficulties, which makes these neglectful families stand out from others in similar material circumstances. It is this 'something' which we need to capture. We do no service to the families if we back away.

This chapter is based on two premises: first, that we should not seek to understand the problems of neglectful parents solely in terms of external pressures on them, but rather in terms of individual and family dynamics, with external pressures as (often powerful) contributing factors. Second, and most particularly in cases of neglect, our attempt to understand and intervene effectively will need a framework wide enough to encompass a wide range of emotional and psychological considerations. If we fail to adopt such an approach, we find ourselves, intellectually and professionally, in a blind alley, in which we cannot progress ideas. However, this attempt is not without difficulties and dangers. For these issues are caught up in the cross currents of ideological differences, of social scientific dispute and of professional rivalries, leaving the less experienced workers unsupported and exposed. They are also extremely complex, especially if one wishes to be pragmatic and eclectic, taking from difference theories or areas of knowledge what seems to be useful. Yet this may be exactly the best way; as Jung put it: 'One could as little catch the psyche in a theory as one could the world. Theories are not articles of faith; they are either instruments of knowledge and or therapy or they are no good at all.'

Characteristics of the families

This chapter seeks to identify certain key issues or characteristics which research and professional experience have identified as recurring and significant in these families and which have clear implications for strategies of intervention. As such, they merit clearer thought and more practice attention than has been given. These issues are:

- 'Neglect' is usually seen in terms of the *mother's* failure to provide care.
- Low self esteem is consistently shown to be a dominant feature of the women's personalities.
- There is little understanding of the reasons underlying the very poor hygiene found in some neglectful families.
- We know very little about the men in these families.
- The physical health status of the parents, especially the mothers, has received little attention.
- The differential impact which particular children make on their parents, in terms of personalities, needs and problems, has been little considered.
- Attention has been drawn to those parents, usually mothers, with learning disabilities who fall into this neglectful group. But the implications of this need sensitive exploration.

Most discussion of neglect centres upon the behaviour of mothers. In drawing attention to their failures, in physical and emotional care and in supervision, we fall into one of the many pitfalls in this discussion, which well illustrates the other ideological tensions lying just under the surface. We reinforce the impression of maternal responsibility for damage to children which has been justly criticised by those who see in this a disregard of men's failure to participate adequately in parenting in families with problems. Farmer and Owen (1995) comment with feeling on this aspect of their findings: 'The focus of mothers pervaded all aspects of the child protection system' (p. 319). They point out that whether the abuse was committed by a man or a woman, the focus of responsibility was on the women, 'who were seen as more amenable and available for intervention' (p. 319). They describe the focus on mothers as 'relentless' and urge that the risks to children should be 'disaggregated' so that practitioners take more account of the particular person from whom a child is at risk (p. 319). They also comment that: 'In most cases of neglect and emotional abuse there was a general assumption that mothers were responsible for all deficits in the case' (p. 318).

Sympathetic as one may be to this point of view, its practical application in the cases with which we are concerned is limited. If mothers are, in fact, the main caretakers in the majority of cases of neglect, then failure to offer appropriate care or to protect children from others is inevitably attributed to them and will be the focus of day-to-day work. However, such work can be underpinned by awareness of, and sensitivity to, the significance of the mothers' feelings about, and experiences of, relationships between men and women, fathers and mothers, especially in relation to the upbringing of children. Most neglectful mothers will have had oppressive experiences with men. There are two dimensions likely to be important. First, the mother's own experiences of 'being fathered'; second, her relationships with men in adult life. Not surprisingly, there is often a connection between the two. The central question which has to be addressed is the effect of past and present experiences with men on the mother's perception of herself and hence on her capacity to nurture and protect her children. A lesser but important question concerns the mother's perception of what men's roles should be in relationship to caring for children. Seeking to find the answers to these questions can lead to imaginative strategies for change – often in the direction of raising self esteem in such women. It will, on occasion, and sadly, point to the extreme difficulties a mother may have in protecting her children from dangerous men. Where there are relatively stable couples amongst neglectful families (and there are a few) an exploration of gender roles may facilitate better adaptation to the children's care. (Perhaps this is most likely in the case of couples where one or both partners have learning disabilities.)

Gaudin's (1993) summary of current knowledge about neglect (see Chapter 2), identifies a number of critical dimensions. The first of these concerns the developmental history of the parents themselves. It will come as no surprise to practitioners to learn that neglectful parents were growing up in unstable, hostile, non nurturing homes which led to unstable personalities when the children become adults, which in turn led to stressful marriages and abusive parenting practices to children (p. 12). As we have seen earlier, such familiar stories, however, are not necessarily effectively utilised by practitioners in terms of assessment and intervention. Indeed, one of the aims of this book is to extract the significance of such knowledge for those who do the work.

Gaudin draws attention to the value of attachment theory in understanding the effects of past events on parenting capacity. This body of theory has been the subject of extensive general research and scrutiny on both sides of the Atlantic. Howe (1995) has valuably explored its implications for social work practice and summarised

(1997) its implications for children's well-being. Rigorous examination by, amongst others, Rutter and Rutter (1993) led to a conclusion in which we can have confidence:

'It seems that the postulate that a lack of continuity in the loving committed parent child relationships is central has received substantial support. What has stood the test of time most of all has been the proposition that the quality of parent child relationships constitutes a central aspect of parenting, that the development of social relationships occupies a crucial role in personality growth and that abnormalities in relationships are important in many types of psychopathology.'

(pp. 341 and 361)

Others have examined specifically neglectful parents in this theoretical context, notably Egeland (1988a; 1988b), and have found connections between unstable attachments in childhood and later parenting difficulties. However, the nature of these connections is – and perhaps will always be – somewhat uncertain as is the evidence on the notion of intergenerational 'cycles' of neglect, in which the debates are strikingly similar to those concerning 'cycles of deprivation' in the 1970s and 1980s (Fuller & Stevenson 1983). Whilst, as Gaudin (1993) points out, numerous studies do suggest a cycle of neglect, 'the direct cause–effect relationship between parental history of neglect and subsequent neglect of children is not clearly established' (p. 13).

Such tidy causal relationships should no longer be expected in the fields with which we are here concerned. Indeed, the uncertainty leads us to a less deterministic view of human nature, as well as a recognition of what Gaudin describes as 'important mediating factors': . . .

'Victims of neglect who do not repeat the cycle have fewer stressful life events; stronger, more stable and supportive relationships with husbands and boyfriends; physically healthier babies'. . .

They are also

'less likely to be maltreated by both parents and more apt to have reported a supportive relationship with one parent or with another adult. *These mediating factors provide critical indicators for improving parents' potential* [my italics].'

(p. 13)

The message from the research, then, is reasonably clear. On the one hand, it makes no sense (indeed it makes *nonsense*) to divorce the past from the present in reflection about the experiences of neglectful parents, especially in their childhood. Indeed, 'personal identities and a sense of belonging form within our relationship history' (Howe 1997). On the other hand, many recent or present experiences, whether in relationships or in life events or situations, may tip the balance one way or another. Such a conclusion is vague but that vagueness is at once both more hopeful and more important than definitive causal links. For it affirms the necessity for those working with the families, first, to look for connections between past and present which are meaningful to the individuals concerned; for example, a mother's perception that she was not cherished as a child has a more direct bearing on work with her than 'the facts' of her deprivation. Second, it encourages a model of work which seeks to build on recent and present strengths and good experiences in the confidence that they can make a difference.

Not surprisingly, studies of neglectful parents have also highlighted a range of characteristics which have been described in terms of personality traits. However, Pianti *et al.* (1989), in their review of aetiological factors in child maltreatment, comment that:

> 'Recently, investigations have turned to examining parental characteristics that are more directly tied to mothers' thoughts and feelings about caretaking rather than measuring static personality traits ... which at best may have only a hypothetical link to caretaking skills... These studies have begun to demonstrate rather consistently that one characteristic differentiating maltreating from adequate caretakers is their lack of understanding of the complexity of social relationships, especially caretaking and their feelings about meeting the needs of another person.'

> (p. 205)

Pianti *et al.* are not here specifically examining neglect, but maltreatment more generally. Other studies have found, however, that neglectful mothers lack knowledge of, and empathy for, children's age-appropriate needs and have more unrealistic and more negative expectations of their children than non neglecting parents (see Jones & McNeely 1980). Thus the direct line between the past and the present would seem to be reinforced. It raises important questions as to whether and how such difficulties can be addressed. We shall return to this in later chapters.

Research on the presence of clinical depression in neglectful mothers is also discussed by Gaudin (1993). The findings are inconclusive, although one study (Zuragin 1988) is cited as showing that, using standardised ratings, 60% of neglectful mothers were significantly depressed compared with 33% of a group in a comparable low income group. Gaudin (1993) rightly concludes that 'such a diagnosis should be considered when assessing child neglect' (p. 14), not least because of the implications it may have for a measure of relief through medication. However, it is probably more useful to think not only in terms of a specific psychiatric disorder, but in terms of the idea of 'low self esteem' which, as suggested earlier, is pervasive in the descriptions of such women. For although low self esteem is a feature of depression, it can exist without the conventional signs of depression. Whilst many factors can and do contribute in adult life to this poor rating of oneself, some neglectful mothers convey a powerful sense that they have not been cherished or nurtured themselves in their formative years. Every dimension of care for the self may be affected by this:

> 'If I am not loved, then I am not worthy of love. It follows that there is no point in seeking to make myself attractive to others, either through appearance or responses. Even my house can be dirty like me; my children, who are, after all, bits of me, need not (cannot) be cherished. As for men, they are allowed to exploit me; maybe because this is how men always were in my family or because I do not deserve anything better.'

It will, of course, not always be as bleak or pervasive as that. But the worker has to make the leap of imagination, based on, and informed by, clear observation, to feel the despair and hopelessness which lies in the hearts of some neglectful mothers. It is essential for realistic, as well as compassionate, strategies to raise self esteem. Without it, in such cases, the endless cycle of advice, practical aid, 'sending in the dirty squad to clean up', is doomed to failure. Meanwhile, the children suffer grievously.

However, important as the deeper reason for low self esteem may be in certain cases, it is frequently reinforced by 'failure' in the here and now. That failure has been described in terms of a deficit in social skills. In relation to the care of children, this may suggest a different model for understanding which has been interestingly explored by Crittenden (1993). She argues that

> 'although neglect clearly results from a nested hierarchy of influences (including social, ecological, family, dyadic attachment), knowledge of internal processes leading to the failure to respond may provide essential information regarding neglectful behaviour'.

>   (p. 28)

Crittenden seeks to integrate developmental theory with cognitive theory and groups neglectful parents in terms of how they *perceive, interpret and respond to information*. She claims that in the approach 'major theoretical perspectives that are often treated as competing are viewed as complementary ... Normative processes, typical of humans, are applied to the case of neglect' (p. 28). She outlines 'four important aspects of neglectful parents' behaviour: perception, interpretation, selection of a response' (p. 29). She argues that, although these distinctions may seem a long way from the usual concerns about neglectful parents' omissions, an understanding of the parents' style of processing information directly contributes to their ability (a) to perceive essential aspects of their children's states, (b) to interpret accurately the meaning of these perceptions, (c) to select adaptive responses and (d) to respond in ways which meet the children's needs (p. 29). Crittenden believes that they may experience reality differently from other parents on any of these dimensions. If this is so, 'simply instructing neglectful parents may be ineffective' (p. 30) (Fig. 5.2).

This way of observing mother–child interactions would seem to have particular value when the children are very young. Crittenden's illustration deals with the responses to crying babies. She shows that, in the first stage of processing, the crying may appear simply not to be heard – 'throwing away the stimulus information'. In the second stage, meaning must be interpreted – what *kind* of crying is this? In the third, a response must be selected: what can be done about it? This involves believing one can take effective action. In the fourth, the response must be implemented, which depends on a range of immediate circumstances and the parents' capacity to meet the child's needs rather than their own (pp. 30–31).

Crittenden develops each of these stages in terms of the particular difficulties of neglectful parents, linking this to existing research. Most

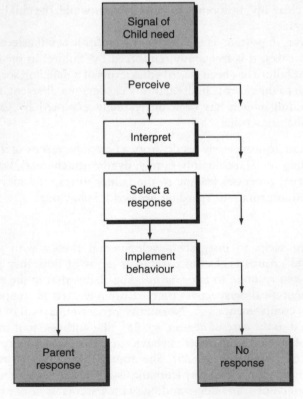

Fig. 5.2 Parental processing of information about child behaviour.

importantly, she discusses the implications for treatment. Her approach has been considered here in some detail, not simply for its intrinsic, substantive interest but because it shows a way of sharpening up the individual observations which must lie at the root of useful assessment. It also emphasises the interactional nature of parent–child ties, an issue which has also been extensively explored by Mass (1996). Mass writes:

'parenting is inherently interpersonal, a person is a parent only in relation to another. Nevertheless, the parental experience, in particular the experience of parents of infants, has been conventionally defined as an intrapersonal, not as an interpersonal phenonomen.'

(p. 425)

Once it is accepted that from birth the infant is capable of entering into two way communication, an observation can be based on interactional behaviour. Mass examines to what parents attribute the behaviour of their child. For example, there can be attributions which are made to the infant's characteristics or to his intentions. 'He was a premature baby. All premature babies cry a lot.' Or 'he cries to irritate me'. Mass' work is conceptually complex and cannot be explored here in depth but, as with Crittenden, it opens the door on *present interaction* as a basis for understanding the situations in neglectful families. As children grow older, the power of interactional factors becomes more readily apparent. The work described here, however, enables 'signals' of parent–child dynamics to be picked up at a very early stage. In cases of neglect, this may be of particular importance.

Thus far, then, in seeking to understand neglectful parents, we have moved from consideration of links between past and present to a range of ways in which the present situation may be viewed, of which, in my opinion, 'diagnostic' categorisation is the least helpful. However, it must also form part of assessment whether one sees this in terms of cause or effect. For example, the literature reports a significant association between substance abuse and neglectful families. There may be cultural variations in the extent of these particular problems. Savage (1994), for example, reported that, in Ireland, 75% of her sample of neglecting mothers had shown evidence of alcohol abuse. (This is higher than in some other studies.) Gaudin (1993) reported various studies which support the association in terms of both alcohol and drugs, but concluded that 'in spite of these associations, there is as yet insufficient data to conclude that substance abuse causes neglect but it is an increasingly significant factor' (p. 15).

Certainly, substance abuse creates serious financial problems which impact on the children. It is also, of course, significant in other kinds of maltreatment, but it may be particularly problematic in terms of the reliable supervision which young children need and, in alcoholism especially, it may play a part in 'intermittent' neglect when there are drinking bouts. Indeed, in a case which featured in my own research concerning neglect (Stevenson 1995), the (lone) mother was reported to offer excellent care between these bouts and to be almost a 'model' mother. Thus a great deal of the professionals' time was spent on finding ways in which to protect the children from harm when the bad patches occurred. Crucial to this was a reliable 'alarm' system, triggered by mother or children, by which protective services (including the grandmother) could be put in place. This was successful and reminds us that the existence of serious problems such as alcoholism does not necessarily carry with it an assumption of the kind of emotional deprivation in parents we have earlier discussed. If that were so, mothering 'between times' could not have been so successful. Much more research is needed, however, on the implications of drug addiction for successful child rearing and, in particular, for intervention in cases of neglect.

Early in this chapter, the centrality of the mother to our discussion was acknowledged, as were the difficulties of this stance. In what followed, I have, wherever possible, considered 'parental' rather than maternal characteristics and interactions only in relation to the neglect of children. Nonetheless, we must accept and discuss the significance of gender and relationships between women and men in such families. Most studies and practitioners report that very large numbers of the families in question are headed by 'lone mothers' or have men 'passing through' in varying degrees of intimacy and stability (Coohey (1995) however did not find this in her USA study). In cases in which there is a quasi-permanence, there are often serious mental and associated problems. Egeland (1988a), in a longitudinal mother–child study, found that an intact, stable relationship with a husband or partner was critical in distinguishing mothers who ceased to maltreat from those who did not. Savage (1994) reported on an Irish study, in which 80% of mothers in the neglecting group had poor relationships with partners: this was the most significant association in her study. As noted earlier, Wilding and Thoburn (1997) reported that 17% of child protection referrals for neglect involved 'extreme spouse abuse'.

The problem, then, is clear; it seems that very few neglectful mothers are well supported by partners and a substantial number of mothers are subjected to severe abuse themselves. There has been, of late, amongst British professionals, mounting evidence of, or anxiety about, the impact of 'domestic' violence on the children as well as the mothers. Analysis of the problem, however, takes us into the area of ideological conflict; if emphasis is placed on the mother's part in getting into, and staying in or repeating such relationships, there are fears that this will reinforce a 'mother blaming' slant which, yet again, deflects responsibility from where it should rightly belong. Yet it is apparent that 'structural' explanations alone, of the difficulties women have in material and practical terms in escaping from unsatisfactory and

damaging relationships, are not sufficient (although clearly con-
tributory) to explain the prevalence and recurring nature of these difficulties. One crucial factor, as we have seen, is low self esteem;
sometimes sinking into a downward spiral of relationship failure,
involving 'the wrong' choices of men in the first place and then, not
uncommonly, the inability of two people to give and to receive, in some
kind of balance, to their mutual benefit. Many of the women and men
involved in these families are unemployed. Such men are particularly
vulnerable to unemployment if jobs are hard to come by and are caught
by low pay and the poverty trap. Women, in addition to such difficulties, have the familiar problems of child care. As we saw in Chapter
3, material problems can be crushing. However, in the context of this
discussion, we need also to understand the effects of unemployment in
creating the sense of being devalued in the individuals concerned, not
infrequently linked to longstanding failure in the educational system.
Research, for example, into the incidence of illiteracy in the parents of
neglected children might show it to be disturbingly high. Such issues
take us into the areas of social exclusion and of marginalisation in
which neglectful parents are only a small sub group. But this reminds us
of the intertwined and interacting model for understanding which we
have adopted.

One important matter has been little discussed, in the context of child
maltreatment, namely, the physical health of parents, especially
mothers, which bears on their capacity to act as effective caregivers and
caretakers of their children. Physical health cannot in fact be separated
from other dimensions. Blackburn (1991) offers a helpful way of
connecting poverty and health, in terms of the processes 'by which
poverty may influence a person's susceptibility to a disease or condition' (p. 44). She suggests that there are three intertwined processes –
physiological, psychological and behavioural.

On the first of these, she cites much evidence to show the direct
connections between poor diet and ill health and poor housing conditions and ill health. Less familiar than the work on diet is the research
on housing conditions. For example, Blackburn cites Platt *et al.* (1989),
whose research on damp, cold and mould in housing conditions
showed increased ill health, such as allergic reactions and respiratory
infections. Although the most serious effects of this are found in children, the impact on adults should also be considered. This study also
shows that physical symptoms in turn affect emotional behaviours,
classically in parents described as having 'bad nerves'.

Blackburn discusses the second of these processes – psychological –
in terms of the way poverty brings with it relative powerlessness and
lack of control over events: 'The daily experience of poverty does little
to foster a sense of being in control' (p. 45). She cites experiences of the
social security system which reinforce feelings of powerlessness, but
could well be applied to the health care system, in particular primary

health care, so that the problem, as it were, doubles back on itself – physical health problems are not addressed or, to combat stress, habits such as heavy smoking are adopted which in themselves damage health.

This leads onto the third, behavioural dimension. In the complex situations in which poor parents find themselves they may 'have to make health choices that serve to protect one aspect of health or the health of another family member whilst undermining another aspect of health or the health of another person'. These are often classed as reckless choices but 'appear to act as a mechanism for coping with some of the stresses and hardships of poverty' (p. 46). (The examples given include smoking and bottle feeding of babies.)

This discussion, of course, is relevant to many more families than those with whom this book is concerned. It reminds us of the complex but substantial evidence concerning the impact of poverty upon health and the extent of inequalities in health in modern society (Townsend *et al.* 1988). But hard as it bears on many families, it has a particular impact on those who, for a variety of reasons discussed in this chapter, are not well equipped to do battle in an unjust society, especially those whose grip on parenting skills is precarious. It is noticeable in the extensive literature on neglect which has been reviewed here, how few comments there are about physical health and the causes and consequences of physical illness. It would be most valuable if studies in this field were to be conducted, perhaps especially in relation to women's gynaecological well-being. Meanwhile, the professionals, especially social workers, would do a valuable service in ensuring that the question of women's physical health is systematically addressed by those competent to do so when other aspects of family functioning are being assessed.

In doing so, it is helpful to note the evidence (Blaxter & Patterson 1984) that working class women may have lower expectations of health than others in our society. They quote from one respondent:

'After I was sterilised, I had a lot of cystitis, and backache because of the fibroids. Then when I had my hysterectomy I had bother with my waterworks because my bladder had a life of its own and I had to have a repair... Healthwise I would say I'm OK. I did hurt my shoulder – I mean, this is nothing to do with health but I actually now have a disability, I have a gratuity payment every six months ... I wear a collar and take Valium then, just the headaches – but I'm not really off work a lot with it.'

(p. 29)

Finally, in the consideration of 'parenting', I turn to the growing interest in the relationship (if such there be) between the presence of learning disabilities in parents and their capacity to parent, most particularly to offer care and supervision which is 'good enough'. Yet again, as we have seen throughout this chapter, we enter an ideological minefield. The stigmatising, inappropriate and inhumane treatment of generations of people believed to have a degree of learning disability, in which groups there were many whose apparent mental disability resulted from either gross social deprivation or physical and sensory problems, is well known. It is a source of shame to an older generation of professionals and fuels a worthy determination in younger workers that such people should have every opportunity to lead an ordinary family life with their children. The tales which recur, of 'eugenics', of institutionalisation, of sterilisation in the not too distant past further reinforce such determination. In social work education, students are now much more engaged by the idea of work with people with learning difficulties and frequently come to professional training with experience in this field.

There is little doubt that there has been a sea change in the attitudes of many professionals generally to the rights of people with learning disabilities to have and bring up children. A local survey in Nottinghamshire (Collins & Nicholson 1997), in which opinions were sought from clinical and occupational therapists, school and community nurses, health visitors, paediatricians, social workers and support workers, showed that:

- 'Attitudes both toward the issue of parenting and the issue of sexuality in general for people with learning disabilities were remarkably positive.'
- 'Just over 60% agreed or strongly agreed that parents with learning disabilities could be taught the necessary parenting skills and the majority disagreed with the statement "you cannot teach someone to be a good parent".'

(executive summary)

Despite this, there is continuing unease expressed by those whose primary focus is on the rights and needs of the person with a learning disability concerning the approach of professionals towards those who are parents. This is strongly illustrated in the article by Booth and Booth (1993) on lessons for practitioners. They pointed out that there had been at that time 'scant research', most from the USA, on parents with learning difficulties (p. 461). Such as there was had 'focused on just four main areas of investigation: issues of heredity and familial handicap; fertility and family size; parental competence and parenting training and child maltreatment or abuse' (p. 461). They were critical of much of it, including the emphasis on 'problems and failings of parents without ... due attention to their competencies and the more positive side of their experience' (p. 462) and the fact that it had focused almost entirely on mothers. Booth and Booth drew attention to the many other factors both intra- and interpersonal and environmental which affect parental competence. They argued that these factors are as significant in child maltreatment amongst parents with learning disabilities as they are in other groups and that therefore attention to these problems will be as, or more pertinent, than focusing on their learning difficulties *per se*.

'Adequate parenting is not a simple function of intelligence, neither is there a simple relationship between parental competence and child outcome' (p. 466). The prescriptive tone of much of the article and the details of the case histories imply that professional handling of such situations leaves a great deal to be desired. This may indeed be so but, equally, the change in values and attitudes amongst professionals is demonstrable. Indeed, it is these very changes which may lead some workers in child protection to a kind of anxious paralysis, especially in cases of neglect. A combination of human rights ideals and sympathy for such parents, associated with uncertainty as to how much change and development is possible, can lead on occasion to situations manifestly harmful to the children continuing too long. The growing specialisation within social service departments, in particular between adult and children services, tends to reinforce unhelpful identification with *either* the adults *or* their children, on both an organisational and an individual level; this is mirrored in the health and psychiatric services.

There has been growing interest in the UK in the issue of parental competence and learning disability in the last 5 years or so. (See for example, McGaw & Sturmey 1994.) This may well be in part, as Booth and Booth point out, because the number of such parents in the community is steadily increasing. However, parents with only moderate degrees of disability may receive little or no support unless they come to the attention of child welfare services. In that case, until the recent shift of focus towards better services for 'children in need', the near exclusive focus on child protection services meant that the only 'visible' parents with learning disabilities were likely to be those whose children were seriously at risk, rather than those who needed support.

If we are to find a sensible way forward, one question has to be addressed. Is the fact of learning disability seriously relevant to an understanding of parenting deficits or is it an unwarrantable diversion from the many other interacting factors in cases of neglect? That is to say, should it be a *focus* for research and professional intervention? There are two ways of considering this. First, it can be viewed as an additional and contributing factor to difficulties in parenting and thus may be one more element in a downward spiral. In general, higher intelligence may make it easier to solve certain problems; bringing up children in modern society requires a range of skills, by no means all of which, as McGaw and Sturmey (1994) point out, are tied simply to parent–child interaction but require 'parent life skills' (p. 39) such as obtaining resources, both social and material. The more intelligent person (other things being equal) is likely to find this easier. Thus, it is perverse to deny or minimise the significance of this particular characteristic.

However, and secondly, the existence of a learning disability may *of itself* cause certain specific problems in child rearing. This is the area which is more controversial, yet, as Booth and Booth discuss, even when due caution about the attribution of difficulties to learning disabilities is exercised, there remain important issues about the effects of cognitive limitation on parent–child care, interaction and supervision. It seems important to give more sophisticated and detailed attention to this. To regard people with learning disabilities as in any way a heterogeneous group, about whom generalisations can be made, is plainly ridiculous, not least when one is aware of the wide range of reasons for, and the type of, such conditions. It is, however, possible to think in terms of the 'ordinary' requirements for 'good enough' parenting skills and assess the extent to which the deficits in some parents can usefully be seen in terms of cognitive difficulties. It should go without saying that other components of assessment which are customarily investigated should be the same for parents with learning disabilities as anyone else. The work of McGaw and colleagues (1994) has been influential and helpful in this. She has developed the notion of a 'parental skills model', based on 'life skills', family history, available support and resources, which takes into account for such parents many of the factors common to all similar assessments (McGaw and Sturmey 1994). However, we shall need to be clearer about the possible significant elements in cognitive limitation in relation to neglect. Booth and Booth (1993), although expressing caution about the reliability of the findings, cite research showing a number of parenting deficits common in people with learning disabilities. These include:

> 'the failure to adjust parenting styles to changes in their child's development, a lack of verbal interaction with the child, insufficient cognitive stimulation, especially in the area of play, a tendency to overgeneralise instructions, inconsistent use of discipline, a lack of expressed warmth, love and affection.'

> (p. 464)

Clearly such deficits are highly relevant to the problem of neglect. But, as they point out, very few of these studies 'have matched comparison groups to control for other variables, apart from intelligence' (p. 464).

Nonetheless, those descriptions do accord with some of the observations of experienced practitioners and some seem consistent with the nature of the intellectual limitations we are considering, rather than with the more emotionally rooted difficulties. For example, it is plausible to see 'overgeneralising instructions', which may mean inappropriate extrapolation from one situation to another, or 'insufficient cognitive stimulation' in terms of learning disability; whereas 'a lack of warmth' may have a more complex and different aetiology.

It is also important to note the observations of Court (personal communication 1997) that parents with learning disability sometimes have limited knowledge and skills in the provision, as parent, of adequate health care and safety to their children. When to that is added the fact that they are less likely to seek and use professional help than most parents, there is an important pointer to the difficulties there may be in providing good enough protection against health hazards to, and illness in, the children.

More rigorous research and more precise observations will be needed in this area if we are to develop further credible direct connections between specific deficits and effective programmes for skill training in such parents. These are of considerable potential importance as one of the elements in strategies for intervention, especially at an early stage. McGaw and Sturmey (1994) stress that any such programmes will have to be 'varied and tailored' to the idiosyncratic profile of family needs and 'will need to be adapted to take account of the individual learning difficulties'. 'Programmes (for such parents) ... need to be long term, more elaborate and more directive than those offered to other parents' (p. 47).

The style and manner of the teaching is also very important. McGaw's (undated) series of five pamphlets 'I want to be a good parent' is an example of the use of pictures and simple written words to convey practical and some associated emotional advice to parents with learning disabilities. As an aid to face to face contact it offers a concrete way of addressing crucial issues in child rearing. It is also an illustration of the magnitude of the tasks when there are major deficits in the cognitive abilities which, along with emotional and social capacities, play a critical part in parenting. When a practitioner, who is not a specialist, believes that a parent who neglects has a learning disability, the first task is to seek to understand the precise ways in which the disability appears adversely to affect parenting. In discussions with practitioners, they frequently mention three areas of difficulty. One is 'not foreseeing trouble': the 'one step ahead' of ordinary parents, by which they protect the children, seems not to operate well. A second is an inability to manage situations which are diverse and complex, most particularly when a number of children simultaneously require attention. A third difficulty, reinforced by research, referred to earlier, is of a rigidity in thought processes which makes adaptation to changed needs or situations problematic. Practitioners would do a great service to the parents and their children if these and other observations were gathered together and their implications for family support and planning for children were systematically explored.

Conclusions

Previous chapters (3 and 4) have shown the caretakers – in particular the mothers – of neglected children in general to be poor and isolated in their local communities, with complex and unsatisfactory relationships with their wider family networks. This chapter has pointed out the difficulties in, and limitations of, utilising current research and has discussed particular areas of concern for practitioners in working with such parents. It would seem essential that practitioners:

- Seek to understand the meaning of the problematic or unacceptable behaviour to the adult concerned; *for example:* a very dirty house. Meaning: a depressed mother? A mother in poor physical health? A mother overwhelmed by too many young children? A mother who feels dirty and debased herself? All these? Some of these? *For example:* a mother's seeming insensitivity towards a baby crying. Meaning: no experience of being nurtured? Therefore, not understanding that she is needed? Depressed, unable to respond at that time? Uncertainty as to what is needed? Anger towards the child? (Why?)
- Follow through those observations by asking: in the light of what we now understand (in part), can we make a difference to reduce the problematic behaviour? If so, how? By 'talk', practical support or by strategies devised to improve parental functioning?
- At all times, bear in mind the possibility that adults may need medical attention.
- Consider in detail the relevance of a learning disability to parenting capacity.

Chapter 6
The Children

This chapter is focused upon children who are neglected, rather than upon their parents or the wider environment in which the family is situated. In a sense, these children are the *raison d'être* of the book. The chapter will explore, first, the background to a widespread concern that social workers have not observed vulnerable children with sufficient sensitivity and precision. Second, and against an accepted view of children's needs, we shall examine some of the evidence concerning the effects of neglect and of neglect with other abuse on children's development.

The social worker and children

British law places the interests of the child at the centre of decision making in the child welfare services. It is somewhat ironic, therefore, that social workers are in general less comfortable in observing and communicating with children than adults. It is important to reflect upon the reasons why this might be so before considering the particular issues which arise in the case of children who are neglected.

In the early post war days of professional education for 'child care officers', considerable importance was attached to the direct observation of, and rapport with, children. Residential child care placements during training were a required element in the course. In the 1950s, memories of the traumatic effects of evacuation upon wartime children were still fresh and had profoundly affected a group of experts in child development who were predominantly psychoanalytic in orientation. The names on the reading lists of all 'child care officer' students included: Barbara Dockar Drysdale (Principal of the Mulberry Bush School for emotionally disturbed children); Anna Freud, a psychoanalyst whose work concerning young children in wartime nurseries was influential; Melanie Klein, a psychoanalyst who had pioneered the analysis of young children; Susan Isaacs, psychologist and psychoanalyst who had written weekly columns for the magazine *Nursery World*; Clare Winnicott, a psychiatric social worker who had worked with evacuated children; Donald Winnicott, paediatrician and psychoanalyst whose influence on paediatric practice was profound and who in popular broadcasts, coined the phrase 'good enough mothering' which now has general currency.

These people were profoundly influential to a generation of social work educators. At the same time, John Bowlby's work (1951; 1969; 1973; 1980) on bonding and attachment was increasingly being recognised as crucially important to child welfare social work. This was epitomised in films made by James and Joyce Robertson on the impact on a young child of going to hospital (Robertson & Robertson 1953) or of entering residential care at 17 months (Robertson & Robertson 1969). All child welfare social work students (and many others) saw these films. The grief, anxiety and despair of these young children, separated from their caregivers, left an indelible impression on all who saw them – including, it was reported, on the then Secretary for State for Health and Social Services, Sir Keith Joseph. Policy for parents to stay with their children in hospital was shaped by these films. Even after these influences waned, the Tavistock Clinic was a focal point of continuing efforts to demonstrate the value of these approaches, involving close observation of children, for social workers, and other professionals, and maintained a valuable presence even when the general climate became inhospitable (Trowell & Bower 1995).

Gradually, however, the emphasis on direct observation of young children dropped away and no longer received explicit attention in the training of social workers. The emphasis on attention to *detail* in seeking to understand the meaning of a child's behaviour was no longer highly valued. This coincided with an 'information explosion' in the broad areas of activity in social work which posed serious strains and dilemmas for educators in the selection of material for basic training and a growing attention to child protection within that part of the curriculum rather than to child welfare more generally. Paradoxically, however, for reasons discussed below, this concentration on child protection was not accompanied by a clarification of the place of child observation within that sphere of the work. On the contrary, a number of child abuse inquiry reports commented unfavourably on the deficiencies in this sphere, notably that concerning Jasmine Beckford (Beckford 1985). In some ways, its overheated style and harshly censorious tone concerning individuals makes one reluctant to cite it yet again. But the point made is powerful, and the analysis of the case of Paul (The Bridge Consultancy 1995), who was neglected, unfortunately suggests that the lesson has still not been learnt.

'Throughout the three years of social work with the Beckfords, Ms Wahlstrom totally misconceived her role as the field worker enforcing Care Orders in respect of two very young children at risk. Her gaze focused on Beverley Lorrington and Morris Beckford; she averted her eyes from the children to be aware of them only as and when they were with their parents, hardly ever to observe their

development, and never to communicate with Jasmine on her own.
The two children were regarded as mere appendages to their parents
who were treated as the clients. (In the meticulous record of nearly
100 pages of detailed notes kept by Ms Wahlstrom and others in the
social worker's report there is not a single entry devoted exclusively
to Jasmine and Louise.)'

(p. 293)

Ten years later, the report on Paul comments:

'We have already indicated that we are alarmed at the lack of entries
in records which show what the children were saying or thinking
about their situation. There was information, of course; perhaps
there are two issues that need to be addressed. First, when information is available it needs to be taken seriously and evaluated; for
example, the concerns that we have already referred to in relation to
the children being dirty and smelly.

Helping children to communicate difficulties, wishes and feelings
is a skilled task which should be part of the social work and police
role within the child protection process. When faced with these kinds
of signals it was important to interview the children within the child
protection procedures, to establish how they saw life within the
family. The word interview has a rather formal ring to it. However,
there are now very many creative ways of enabling children to
express their views, their wishes and their feelings. It is possible to use
art, play, drama, children's stories and computers to enable children
to express their views. As far as we can judge, prior to Paul's death
and excluding the incidents relating to suspected sexual abuse,
attempts at obtaining the children's views were very limited.

We cannot stress too highly how important it is, when dealing with
families who are in touch with Social Services, that there is a clear
methodology which allows for skilled, creative discussions with
children and young people. They are living the experience and can
give a more accurate picture of what life is like in a family than any
assessment made externally by a professional.'

(pp. 171–2)

More recently, continuing variations, rather than general weaknesses,
in this area of practice are highlighted in Farmer and Owen (1995).
They contrast, with examples, (p. 221) social workers' descriptions of
appropriate and sensitive work with children and work which has
echoes of the earlier practices described above. More generally, the
difficulty which there has been in incorporating children's perspectives
through their participation in case conferences further illustrates the
strange, contradictory situation in which we have found ourselves.

There have been welcome indications that this problem is now being more generally addressed. A number of social work courses have reintroduced child observation; the publication by the Central Council for Education and Training in Social Work (CCETSW) (Bridge & Miles 1996) of collected essays on the observation of young children is one of the most recent examples of a shift in emphasis. But what led to this apparently obvious gap in practice, which lasted so long? There would appear to be three interlocking strands.

The first concerns the consequence of the association which was described above of child observation with psychoanalytic theory. We have earlier discussed the pervasive effects of a sociological critique of social work which accused the profession of using individualistic explanation of their clients' problems to avoid consideration of, and action on, social problems. As psychoanalytic theory and its derivatives were jettisoned, so social workers were left without working theories for use with children, who got sidelined in the wider ideological debate. Even theory such as that used in behavioural approaches, which bore no relation to psychoanalysis (Jehu *et al.* 1972) did not find much favour in the ideological climate of the time. Such was the power of a prevailing sociopolitical analysis. The lack of an acceptable theoretical basis for work with children partly accounts for social workers' loss of confidence in their capacity to perform this part of the work and loss of conviction in its importance. Indeed it may well be that an increasing trend towards the use of 'experts' in court cases reflects this insecurity.

However, this theoretical vacuum is not the only factor in this skill deficit. Two other closely related factors came into play during the period we are considering. The first concerns role definitions and the second, the shift to the forensic model of practice which we have discussed in Chapter 1. During the period when many social workers in child protection seemed to stop noticing children, their colleagues, in long term teams and in voluntary agencies concerned with fostering and adoption, were busy developing creative work with children, much of it derived from the very same psychoanalytic or related theory, notably that surrounding the concept of 'attachment' (see for example Aldgate & Simmonds 1988). They doggedly pursued such approaches, often in an organisational and professional climate which was unsympathetic.

Furthermore, the weaknesses described above were much less evident in the work of staff in family centres. Indeed, staff from varying backgrounds in these centres, such as teachers, had little difficulty (to put it simply) in 'noticing' children's behaviour. However, neither did many of the social workers in the same setting. It is clearly not *sui generis*! Nor can it be generally attributed to the 'youth' of social workers, a large number of whom were middle aged parents. Not for the first time, we must look to the rather alarming impact of role expectations and reinforcement within field settings for an explanation.

It would seem that the effect of the trend towards a forensic model of child protection, which laid great stress on the investigation of 'incidents' or 'happenings', deflected workers in investigative roles away from the more holistic and integrated view of children and their developmental needs which is needed to access neglect. The management of sexual abuse investigations both confuses and confirms this analysis. Intensive interviewing by police and social workers together, for 'disclosure', has highlighted the difficulties in which the forensic approach has placed child protection workers. In these interviews, play materials are used and children watched and listened to carefully. Yet these 'forensically directed' interviews have not redressed the balance. Within their own framework, concerned with legal process and evidence, the specialist police are often better trained than the social workers. Because the latter lack this background, but also any other sound theoretical framework on which to base their work, this results sometimes in an inbalance of power between the two professions. Most serious, the nature and extent of therapeutic work with children before court hearings, and the skills required to practise it, have been seriously hindered by legal require-ments. The ramifications of this cannot be explored here but, in the context of this analysis, it adds to what we may describe as 'the skill' deficit work with children (Department of Health 1994).

That which is lost can be found. A number of trends, including the 'refocussing initiative' in this decade, suggest a more rounded appraisal of children will be part of the new culture. It will, however, have to be supported by management structures, especially supervision, which affirm its importance for *all* workers within the child welfare social work. The incorporation of the broad principles of the *Looking after Children* materials (Department of Health, Appendix IX) into depart-mental policy and practice, both for 'looked after' children and for children in their own families, is a significant step. These materials also remind us that the earlier extended discussion about social work and children does not in any way detract from the vital part played by other disciplines in the task of appraising the well-being of children, which may often be more important than the contribution of social workers in the areas where certain kinds of expertise are needed. Yet the ines-capable fact remains that where abuse and neglect are evident or sus-pected, the social worker visiting the home is in a key role. That role does not usually extend into specifically 'therapeutic' activity. But it can, and sometimes should, go well beyond the rather detached notion of 'observation' because both assessment, initial and ongoing, and intervention involve interaction. As Trowell and Miles point out:

'The observational stance requires them to be aware of their envir-onment, the verbal and non verbal interaction; to be aware of their own responses as a source of invaluable data, provided they're aware of what comes from them and what from their clients.'

(in Bridge & Miles 1996, p. 41)

The CCETSW publication (Bridge & Miles 1996) referred to above usefully draws attention to the learning which can follow from systematic child observation, as illustrated in Fig. 6.1. This accords well with the ecological model for understanding suggested in Chapter 2 (Fig. 2.1).

'Observation' should, of course, include direct communication with the children themselves. The Bridge Consultancy (1995) remind us that the children have a story to tell. After Paul's death one of the children made a statement to the police 'covering her perception of her life with the family' (pp. 171–2). It makes grim reading, and, as the report points out, she might not have been prepared to do so before the tragedy. However, the report 'cannot stress too highly how important it is ... that there is a clear methodology which allows for skilled creative discussions with children and young people. They are living the experience'. Therein lies another reason (sometimes) for the avoidance of direct contact with children. As Trowell and Miles (in Bridge & Miles 1996) highlight: 'By the very nature of their task, social workers

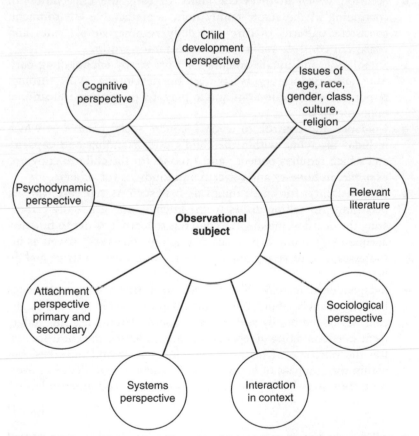

Fig. 6.1 Some of the range of learning that can follow observation (Bridge & Miles 1996, p. 126).

are constantly asked to work with acutely painful situations' (p. 41). The pain of children is particularly hard to bear and that of chronically neglected children is in a class of its own.

What do we need to notice?

The basic needs of children as outlined by Cooper (1985) have stood the test of time well. They are used in the guide to comprehensive assessment (Department of Health 1988 – the 'orange book').

- 'Basic physical care: which includes warmth, shelter, adequate food and rest, grooming (hygiene) and protection from danger.
- Affection: which includes physical contact, holding stroking, cuddling and kissing, comforting, admiration, delight, tenderness, patience, time, making allowances for annoying behaviour, general companionship and approval.
- Security: which involves continuity of care, the expectation of continuing in the stable family unit, a predictable environment, consistent patterns of care and daily routine, simple rules and consistent controls and a harmonious family group.
- Stimulation and innate potential: by praise, by encouraging curiosity and exploratory behaviour, by developing skills through responsiveness to questions and to play, by promoting educational opportunities.
- Guidance and control: to teach adequate social behaviour which includes discipline within the child's understanding and capacity and which requires patience and a model for the child to copy, for example, in honesty and concern and kindness for others.
- Responsibility: for small things at first such as self care, tidying playthings, or taking dishes to the kitchen, and gradually elaborating the decision-making the child has to learn in order to function adequately, gaining experience through his mistakes as well as his successes, and receiving praise and encouragement to strive and do better.
- Independence: to make his own decisions, first about small things but increasingly about the various aspects of his life within the confines of the family and society's codes. Parents use fine judgement in encouraging independence, and in letting the child see and feel the outcome of his own poor judgement and mistakes, but within the compass of his capacity. Protection is needed, but over-protection is as bad as too early responsibility and independence.'

(p. 31)

It will be readily apparent that each one of these is of potential importance for neglected children; as Cooper points out, these needs are met intuitively by 'good enough parents' and they apply to all cultures. Thus, before we begin to elaborate, refine or attempt any kind of measurement, we can do much by simply, but systematically, addressing these issues. They also give the framework for giving guidance, perhaps to sceptical courts by detailed examples of the overarching concepts. There is now very considerable general evidence of developmental harm caused by abuse and neglect. No research can predict conclusively (except in physically gross cases) the long term harm to individuals whose characteristics and subsequent life events will affect outcomes. But one can, in general, point to likely consequences of maltreatment and it is perverse to think only, or mainly, of demonstrable physical/sexual injuries.

Gaudin (1993), in his review of research, concluded that 'child neglect can have devastating effects on the intellectual, physical, social and psychological development of children'. However, he added that: 'studies of maltreated children often fail to differentiate between abused and neglected children' (p. 19). This issue, however, has been addressed in recent studies, including some published before Gaudin's review, and these are drawn on extensively here. The Bridge Consultancy (1995) report on Paul sets out a list of indicators which form a background to the detailed discussion which follows:

'Babies and children who are physically and emotionally neglected are at high risk of suffering:

- gross under stimulation
- failure to thrive, which can lead to poor growth, developmental delay and, in an extreme form, death
- disturbances in emotional attachment
- language delay
- conduct disorder
- poor educational performance
- severe nappy rash and other skin infections
- recurrent and persistent minor infections

As they grow older they will feel

- unloved and unloving
- powerless and hopeless
- a severe lack of self esteem
- isolated from peers and adults'

(p. 3)

Pioneering work differentiating neglect from other forms of abuse was undertaken by Egeland, Sroufe and colleagues. Their two studies (1981; 1983) distinguished four patterns of maltreatment: physically abusive, hostile/verbally abusive, psychologically unavailable and neglectful. These patterns were used to investigate developmental outcomes. In the first study, a striking finding was that there was a pattern of declining function of maltreated children, especially in the 'psychologically unavailable' group. These difficulties had become apparent by 12 months and were clear by 18 months. Of those classed as 'neglected', a 'significantly higher proportion of neglected children were "anxiously attached", at 12 and 18 months, than the control group'.

These findings were used as a basis for the second study of preschool children up to 4 and 5 years. They found that, in general, all four maltreatment groups 'continued to function poorly and were well below their age mates from similar backgrounds but who did not have a history of abuse' (p. 468). 'However, there were considerable differences between the four groups. Physically abused children were the most distractible and non compliant' (p. 468). But it is the findings of the 'psychologically unavailable' and neglected groups which were the most striking. Most disturbingly, the former children exhibited 'a large number of pathological behaviours'. These include: 'unusual sexual behaviours; wetting or soiling, excessive appetite, repetitive movements such as rocking and self punishing behaviours' (p. 465). The overall picture was a sorry one. The neglected children

> 'appeared to have difficulty in pulling themselves together to deal with tasks... They were the least flexible and creative in attempts to solve (a particular) task. Children in the neglect without physical abuse group received the lowest ratings in both self esteem and agency (i.e. appropriate confidence and assertiveness). These same children were also the most dependent and demonstrated the lowest ego control in the pre school.'

> (p. 469)

No subsequent research (for example: Crouch & Milner 1993; Ney *et al.* 1994) has findings which challenge the general thrust of this work. Rather, studies have elaborated and developed this gloomy picture. The early studies by Egeland *et al.* (1988a; 1988b) took into account the interaction of some different types of maltreatment which can obviously co-exist. Thus, physical abuse, with or without neglect and vice versa, were also measured. It appears, however, that the possibility of combined 'psychological unavailability and neglect' was not taken into account in their studies and that neglect was defined more narrowly, in terms of 'irresponsible and incompetent managing of child care activities' (p. 462), than we are here considering. Thus, in reporting the findings, I have assumed the category of 'psychological unavailability' of mothers is likely to be in some cases a part of a neglectful pattern. The combination of the two strengthens the possibility of powerfully adverse consequences for the child.

Most of the research which has been reviewed above concerns the extensive and far reaching consequences of neglect upon the children's social and emotional development. However, concentration upon these subtle and complex matters should not lead us to minimise the serious effects of physical neglect *per se*. Cooper's (1985) outline of the needs of children puts basic physical care at the top of the list but passes over it briefly: 'warmth, shelter, adequate food and rest, grooming, (hygiene) and protection from danger'. Perhaps she thought 'it is so obvious'. Indeed, yet how is it that a stage can be reached when, by any standards, a child or children are not receiving sufficient care to meet these basic needs and yet action has not been taken? The case of Paul (The Bridge Consultancy 1995) starkly reminds us of the tragic consequences of physical neglect. Paul, aged 18 months, 'had lain in urine soaked bedding and clothes for a considerable number of days'. (He had) 'burns over most of his body derived from the urine staining plus septicaemia with septic lesions at the ends of his fingers and toes. In addition, he was suffering from severe pneumonia' (p. 7).

Such cases are thankfully rare and inquiries afterwards demonstrate that complex interacting factors, both in family behaviour and inter-agency co-operation, all play a part in the ultimate tragedy. However, in the context of this discussion, the lesson, over and over again, is the need to focus attention on the detail of the care being offered and to be aware that, in cases of neglect, we may be on a slippery slope, in which 'more or less' good enough parenting slips to 'not good enough' and thence to 'quite inadequate'. It is this 'slippery slope' which has posed so many difficulties in taking decisions and to professional relief when there is an 'incident'. There are basic norms of development to guide professionals, such as the percentile charts, and it is indefensible for these not to be utilised. The Bridge Consultancy report notes that some of the older children in Paul's family had been described from baby-hood onwards as 'grossly overweight'. 'Such a condition can be as much an indicator of neglect as where a child fails to thrive' (p. 173).

In the end, judgements as to whether physical care is 'good enough' must be taken on the basis of an assessment of its various components by the agencies and professionals qualified to do so. Whilst there may be some difficult questions concerning differing cultural or class standards by which these matters should be judged (Chapter 4), these can be overstated in matters of basic physical care. Indeed, one suspects that such debates can serve as a diversion from the more important questions as to why serious physical neglect has been so difficult to address satisfactorily.

It is pertinent also to consider the place of food and feeding within the context of physical care, as well as its deep emotional significance. There are examples of children who, quite simply, do not get enough food of any kind and are hungry. The reasons for this, however, are very varied. There may be problems of managing on a low income; as indicated in Chapter 3, there are many families living – or trying to live

– on an income well below the official poverty line. Such problems, linked sometimes to lack of understanding of nutritional needs, should always be the first point of exploration.

However, this by itself is not sufficient to understand the reasons underlying nutritional difficulties. The extensive research (Skuse 1985) conducted concerning non organic 'failure to thrive' indicates that such children do indeed fail to get enough calories to sustain development. But the patterns of interaction which can be observed between parents and their young children suggest a wide range of behaviours leading to the problem. It is important that we include neglected children and their mothers in such observations, rather than putting them in a class apart, bearing in mind that attitudes to food, feeding and being fed are bound up with past and recent, good and bad, experiences. It is also basic to our understanding of the situation that a hungry child is an anxious child and that experiences of hunger carried forward have profound effects through childhood to adult life on subsequent behaviour. What is it like to be hungry, day after day, week after week, month after month?

A further dimension concerning physical health which is of great significance in cases of neglect concerns inattention to children's medical needs and problems. Some child protection procedures refer to this specifically as an element of neglect; for example, the Nottinghamshire (1997) procedures refer to 'children whose parents/carers are failing or refusing to seek medical advice or treatment'. There are many examples, both in published reports or inquiries and in internal reviews following child deaths, of a pattern of missed health appointments. Not all of these relate to serious medical conditions but neglect of children with minor physical problems, such as those connected with hearing and sight, can further reinforce the disadvantage and stigma, particularly at school, from which so many neglected children already suffer. A squint, for example, can prompt mockery and teasing from other children. Whilst caution must be exercised in the weight and significance which is placed on 'missed appointments', taken in conjunction with other elements in neglect, or standing out in their frequency, it is clear that the cumulative impact on the health of children necessitates careful attention.

A further issue to consider is that of intellectual and educational attainment. At a time in the UK when the 'special needs' of children are inadequately served by a competitive ethos in schools and by resource constraints, it is particularly disturbing that studies have shown neglected children to be the most seriously affected educationally of maltreatment children. Kurtz *et al.* (1993a) commented that 'there is a pressing need for well contrived studies that examine the developmental consequences of abuse and neglect on the school aged children' (p. 581). Their study concluded: 'Academic failure emerged as the single and most consistent risk factor for neglected children' (p. 587).

Furthermore, 'the neglect group's rate of absences for the year prior to implementation of the study was nearly five times that of the comparison group' (p. 587). As these authors, and others, point out, this should not surprise us:

> 'Intellectual development depends heavily on the ongoing quality of parent child interaction... Low educational aspirations, lack of encouragement for learning, a lack of language stimulation, non participation in school activities and unresponsiveness to the child's achievement all undermine school success.'

(p. 588)

A particular facet of this to which reference is made in various studies relates to language development, clearly the key to educational attainment (Allen & Oliver 1982; Fox *et al.* 1988). The lack of stimulation in early years which is so characteristic of such families means that the amazing linguistic achievements of this period in normal children are 'dulled'. Small wonder that such children are later found to be 'at extreme risk of school failure' (Kurtz *et al.* 1993(b), p. 100).

Reviews of the evidence on these matters, such as that by Crouch and Milner (1993), rightly draw attention to the limitations of some studies, for example in terms of sample size or bias, and to confusions regarding the definitions of 'neglect' used. But there is a feeling of anger and sadness that the cumulative impact of these studies, when set beside what is known about the necessary conditions for optimal development, has not been more effectively utilised by child welfare services. Put at its crudest, we heap up trouble for the future. As Ney *et al.* (1994) movingly put it:

> 'Our evidence supports the hypothesis that the most severe psychological conflicts arise from neglect. Having been deprived of the necessary ingredients in their normal development, children never seem to accept the loss of a childhood that could have been. They keep searching as adolescents and adults, only to find those they search amongst are usually themselves deprived people who not only cannot provide them with what they needed as children, but also tend to abuse them, partly out of their own frustrations in encountering somebody who they thought would give to them when they are so hungry.'

(p. 711)

Everyone who works with such families will recognise that description.

However, this does not mean that we need to accept the inevitability of such outcomes. There are two important 'corrective' possibilities. One of these, which will be discussed in the last chapter of the book, concerns the potential for constructive preventive and remedial action to avert or ameliorate some of the worst effects of neglect and/or abuse which we have considered here. But there is another vital element which concerns the individual characteristics of the children themselves. They are not little blobs of dough, moulded by the care – or the neglect – of others. They are part of the dynamic system of the family, bringing to it individual strengths as well as weaknesses. These processes begin in the earliest days when intimacy of mother and child (and sometimes also of father and children) is intense. The degree of intensity of response and the ways of reacting to certain stimuli are variable according to the child's personality. Every ordinary parent knows this; it is part and parcel of the unique interaction between these people – this parent and this child. Yet in the files of neglectful families held by social services departments, there is often a lack of differentiation in the descriptions of children. Their parents, in contrast to 'ordinary' ones, themselves may find it difficult to pinpoint the special traits of their children. The children may play a part in this, if their behaviour lacks the distinctiveness and sparkle which characterises most children.

This is a matter on which we have as yet relatively little research, but Crittenden (1992) gives a flavour of what could be further studied in her analysis of 'children's strategies for coping with adverse environments', which examined the issue in relation to four groups of maltreated children including neglected and abused and neglected, and one group of children not maltreated.

This study focused on four aspects of coping: the relationships between coping style and the type of maltreatment; developmental differences in styles of coping; the coherence of the style of coping across different situations and the immediate and long term adaptiveness of alternate styles of coping (p. 329). The study used attachment theory as a theoretical foundation. Her observations on the second and third of these aspects are of particular significance to neglect. Regarding 'coherence of patterns', and drawing on attachment theory, Crittenden pointed out that

> 'the child develops expectations regarding a caregiver's behaviour and his or her own behaviour. These expectations are based on previous experience and function to enable the child to organise his behaviour around the attachment figure.'

> (p. 330)

The idea of a 'coping strategy' is not simply a 'cognitive plan'. It describes an ongoing process by which infants and children usually attempt to resolve problems of interaction without conscious thought. The assumption is that there is a kind of internalised model of how the attachment figure is expected to react.

> 'Neglected children are expected to have models tied to the unresponsive and apparent helplessness of their caregivers and the inef-

fectiveness of their own efforts to elicit care. Their effect is likely to be one of despair. Children who are both abused and neglected experience a less consistent and predictable environment.'

(p. 331)

As a result, such children may be more aggressive in their uncertainty.

Whether or not attachment theory is used to understand such interactions, it is useful to reflect on this notion of expectation of another's behaviour which is 'in the head' and which influences the responses which we make. Clearly, this is part of every day interactions with those we know; the better we know them, the more powerful the reactions are. Fear of provoking violence, for example, in adult domestic violence can lead to all kinds of 'strategies', based not simply on the actual threat but on expectations of it – the image 'in the head'. Crittenden also comments on 'adaptiveness'. Some abused children adopt strategies which are 'short term' adaptive (for example on avoiding physical violence) but 'long term' maladaptive in their impact in mental health. Neglected children 'who cope with an unresponsive environment by withdrawing from people may not benefit in either the short or long term sense' (p. 332).

The study which Crittenden reports cannot be discussed here in the detail it merits, but the findings give an indication of its significance for a better understanding of the range and variety of children's responses to maltreatment. However, the very nature of the research, which is based on conventional empirical quantitative methods and seeks to generalise between the identified groups of maltreated children, denies the researcher the opportunity to comment on the more subtle variation between individual children within such groups. The fact of uniqueness is both morally and practically crucial. Nonetheless, Crittenden's well founded observations on children's reactions to parenting behaviour give a framework within which practitioners can base their assessment of particular children. She notes that:

'abused – and – neglected children had experience with coercion and power; they also had unresponsive mothers. Their behaviour showed less consistency and self control than the abused children's... They were unable to contain their anxiety and anger upon their mother's return.'

(p.339)

'Neglected children showed consistent behaviour across situations: they were the most passive with their mothers ... *The children's coping strategy seemed to be less of a strategy than the lack of one* [my italics] ... Their behaviour was consistent with models of both their own and others helplessness.'

'Only neglected children showed no greater sophistication in coping strategies as a function of age.'

(p. 340)

'They merely substituted increased difficultness for lessened passivity. This, in and of itself, may indicate serious problems.'

(pp. 339–40)

In selecting matters of particular salience to our theme of neglect from the large corpus of work on childrens' development, needs and problems, there remains one issue of particular importance, namely the time frame, known and predictable, within which ordinary children develop, physically, intellectually and emotionally. It is commonplace to remark upon the adverse effects of delay in firm plans for children occasioned by administrative and legal processes. Sadly, despite the compelling case made for this to be addressed, beginning in 1973 with the influential publication of Freud *et al.*, *Beyond the Best Interests of the Child*, recently revised and republished (Goldstein *et al.* 1996), there is plenty of evidence that delay continues to be a major feature of those cases in which the courts become involved. In the matter of sexual abuse, for example, the Social Services Inspectorate (Department of Health 1994) referred to the fact that 'many concerns were expressed at the long delays in bringing cases involving child witnesses to court' (p. 61). However, the problem is by no means limited to sexual abuse or to the involvement of the courts. It is particularly problematic in relation to neglect or less dramatic, but cumulative, incidents of abuse. In these cases, workers often hesitate for long periods as to whether a situation is 'bad enough' even to initiate court action. When they do so, there is often a further period of investigation and attempts to improve the family functioning. The reasons for this are discussed elsewhere in this book, but here we focus on the effects on children of prolonged deficits in parenting at various crucial points and, sometimes, of prolonged insecurity and uncertainty about their future away from their parents. There are many aspects of Goldstein's *et al.*'s recommendations concerning policy on decisions about young children which are contentious, but their analysis of the 'child's sense of time' remains as telling as it was 25 years ago. Of children who are 'waiting' they wrote:

'Unlike adults who have learned, at least in theory – to anticipate the future and thus to manage delay, children have a built in sense based on the urgency of their instinctive and emotional needs... A child gradually develops the capacity to anticipate the future and postpone gratification'

(p. 41)

The authors suggest that time has 'different meanings' for children at each stage of their development. For example, 'an infant or toddler cannot stretch her waiting more than a few days without feeling overwhelmed by the absence of her parents' (p. 41). (Memories are awakened of the Robertson films referred to earlier.) And so the time 'stretches' as the child grows older.

> 'A child may experience a given time period not according to its actual duration, ... but according to her subjective feelings of impatience, frustration and loss ... *Since a child's time is directly related to her capacity to cope with breaches in continuity, it becomes a factor in determining if and with what urgency the law should act* [my italics].
>
> (p. 42)

For many more neglected children, however, the issue is not separation but the continuation of a life at home which does not meet crucial developmental needs at the right times and stages. There is, therefore, a kind of cumulative deficit in which, having missed certain opportunities for nurturing (say, the stimulation at home through play of the toddler years), the capacity to utilise the next stage (say of pre-school or early primary education) is impaired or hindered. Most important of all, the opportunities for stable, reliable and warm attachment grow fewer as the years go by and the child becomes less capable of responding to adults constructively. These observations do not lead us in the direction of hasty planning; above all, every effort should be made to keep children within their families wherever possible. We must, however, regard vacillation and hesitation, a lack of 'grip' in formulating plans, whether for better care at home or for care elsewhere, as a serious omission of care by the formal system which parallels the omission of care by the parents. Every year that is lost in these formative years makes the road to healthy development harder to travel.

Conclusions

We have come then, by a rather long and circuitous route, to sum up the most important messages of this chapter and to consider their implications.

First, we cannot improve work for neglected children without a sea change in the approach to assessment of children's needs and capacities in part by social service departments generally and by social workers individually in the front line of home assessment. Much of this, of course, requires collaborative work with other professionals with particular expertise. But it requires, first, the sharpening of skills of observation so that the right questions are asked. There is some evidence that this may pose particular problems in relation to neglected infants and very young children who may be unnaturally passive, 'good' and 'contented' or both abused and neglected, who may give out confusing messages.

There are heartening indications that the tide is on the turn. But it requires a consistent and co-ordinated approach both in educational institutions and in agencies. It also requires theoretical frameworks within which to place observations, rather than disconnected 'lists' of norms. Perhaps, controversially, it seems to me more important for theories to be used to stimulate workers than to fasten onto a particular theory. Nonetheless, attachment theory, together with proven knowledge concerning child development more generally, has a special value in observation.

Second, the growing evidence of the lasting harm to children, *which must surely be described as 'significant'*, of both neglect and abuse and neglect combined is more than adequate to justify a new emphasis in child welfare practice. Of course, much more research is needed, especially in relation to cultural factors, and there are some reservations concerning the methodological concentration on quantitative modes of research which appears to dominate the American literature. Yet it is politically and professionally irresponsible not to grasp the implications of what has been discovered. Although emotional deficits give rise to much concern in many cases and have all too often been inadequately appraised, the professional neglect of the health and educational problems of neglected children must also be at the forefront of interagency concern.

Third, it is highly regrettable that the known time scales for normal child development, most especially in the early years when the pace and range of development is bewilderingly fast, have not been adequately incorporated into the judicial and administrative systems which have so much power over children in these circumstances. Children 'in limbo' in their own homes are endangered, just as are those 'in limbo' in care.

Finally, the uniqueness of individual children, in terms of their capacities, needs and responses to their situation, must be emphasised. There is a danger that the evidence of harm to which extensive reference has been made in this chapter could become a dead weight, a pessimistic burden on the shoulders of those who have to act to safeguard children. But whilst the evidence can ring alarm bells and can offer new ways of forming and presenting judgements on particular cases, fortunately it cannot predict, with certainty, outcomes for individual children. Innate characteristics (such as buoyancy or high intelligence) and extraneous, external events (such as the contribution of a loving and gifted teacher) can enable singularly unpromising beginnings to be transcended. Spotting what might make a benign difference to *this* child and utilising it is the creative skill which should underpin purposeful planning.

For practitioners, then, there are three essential points to be drawn out concerning neglected children.

- Systematic and detailed, multidisciplinary, direct assessment of such children at home and outside is indispensable: it must include perceptive observation of adult–child interaction.
- The evidence is now overwhelming that at all ages, but especially as they get older, severely neglected children suffer particularly serious developmental delay, often with permanent consequences.
- Waiting for parental care to improve is necessary and fair but there must be limits, carefully set in relation to children's stages of development.

Chapter 7

Agencies and Professionals Working Together on Cases of Neglect

The past 20 years have seen remarkable developments in British systems for child protection, notably in the field of interagency and interprofessional co-operation. It is beyond the scope of this book to explore these developments in detail; we now have a significant 'indigenous' literature on the subject, notably the research studies of Birchall and Hallett (1995) and Hallett (1995) which gave a portrait of 'the state of play' in the early 1990s. The authors drew their evidence from respondents comprising six professional groups: health visitors, general practitioners, paediatricians, police, social workers and teachers. There is also much relevant comment and research concerning specific aspects of child protection involving co-operative activity such as case conferences reviewed by Stevenson (1995). Most of this research does not discuss specifically interprofessional co-operation in relation to neglect. The Birchall and Hallett studies, however, do include specific references to it.

We now understand much more about the complex processes underlying attempts to co-operate across agencies and professions. In my previous work (Stevenson 1989) I suggested that there were a number of dimensions which could be used to explore these processes. These were:

- Structure and systems
- Relative status and perceived power of the parties
- Role identification
- Professional and organisational priorities
- The extent to which co-operation is perceived as mutually beneficial and in what ways
- The dynamics of case conferences
- Differing attitudes towards, and values concerning child abuse and the family'

(p. 175)

All these factors are as relevant to neglect as to other forms of abuse. They form a useful background to the discussion of work with neglectful families, reminding us of the complex factors which will underline efforts to improve this aspect of child protection. However, as we shall later see, research reveals numerous tensions, problems and complexities in interprofessional and interagency work, most of which are salient to cases of neglect and some of which are particularly pertinent to it.

It is remarkable that such effective working relationships across organisational boundaries have been established, not least when the extent of change and resource constraints during the period under review is acknowledged. For all its imperfections, interprofessional co-operation in British child protection work is widely admired by workers in other countries. The necessity of 'working together' has commanded a large measure of agreement and has resulted in energetic efforts in different ways and at different levels to pursue this goal. The foundations on which to build are sound.

However, it is now widely agreed amongst professionals that the political, social and economic climate of the past 20 years has in some ways worked against these efforts, despite continuing exhortations from (inter alia) central government to persist in attempts to improve communication and co-operation in the protection of children. The countervailing trends are well recognised and will not be much expanded here. They are, first, a complex amalgam of organisational change and fragmentation, with an associated emphasis on competition, which has particularly affected three of the key players in child protection, education, health and social services. Second, the emphasis on 'targeting', 'efficiency' and 'value for money', however desirable in itself, has made it harder to justify and sustain innovative work or work whose benefits cannot easily be quantified. Third, (and related), the political philosophy of an earlier administration, which was not disposed to 'interference' in family life, save in grave circumstances, has posed difficulties for the development of preventative work.

All this, and more, has placed a strain on agencies and individuals seeking to work together to protect children and is of particular relevance to neglect and emotional abuse as categories of maltreatment in which the goals and methods of intervention have been less clear, the likely need for longer term work less acceptable to management and the organisational networks especially complex.

There have also been particular strains between, on the one hand, social service departments, and, on the other, health and education agencies which are illustrated by the studies which we shall discuss (Birchall and Hallett 1995; Hallett 1995) but which are not fully discussed in them. We have earlier considered the emergence of the socio-legal, quasi forensic approach in child protection, notably with social services and police agencies. This may clash with the traditional approach of health personnel, especially health visitors to children. The extent to which this became the prevailing discourse in social services departments is only now becoming fully apparent, when efforts are being made to shift the approach of workers to referrals following the refocusing initiative.

A related problem concerns the irritation of the worker, perhaps a health visitor or teacher, who contacts a social worker wishing to 'consult' and finds herself being asked to say whether this is a 'referral' before she is ready to do so. The implication of such an exchange is clear. In the social worker's eyes, the worker should know what she wants to happen; yet the worker may need to share and discuss before making such a judgement. Such difficulties are particularly likely to arise in less precise cases, such as those of neglect, sexual or emotional abuse. In fairness, there is an underlying issue of importance – that the social worker needs to be clear about the status of the information being conveyed. ('What am I supposed to do with this?') There can be confusion when information is passed on 'confidentially' or 'unofficially'. Nevertheless, in various local authorities, we are now seeing changes in procedures that will facilitate consultations before referral. This is likely to be helpful in opening up a dialogue about cases of neglect.

Behind this, and of far ranging importance, are the changes being initiated more generally in referral procedures, in which consideration of whether children are 'in need' or 'in need of protection' will be developed more systematically (Chapter 9). There can be no doubt that many professionals, especially those from health, welcome this shift in policy, which accords with their own perspective, especially in relation to health promotion and prevention programmes. Furthermore, political endorsement can be seen in the renewed emphasis on 'public health', on which a white paper is awaited. There are indications that the role of the health visitor may be extended but also that her services will be required for intensive child and family work where appropriate. This could fit well with a strategy for cases of neglect.

In social services departments, at the time of writing this book, the attitudes of social workers to these changes are ambivalent and vary widely between individuals and localities. It is clear that the personal ideology and value base of many social workers leads them in the same direction as the health professionals. But some other factors tug in a different direction. First, many younger social workers have acquired all their working experience in departments dominated by the 'forensic' approach to child protection and, most important, by an almost exclusive concentration on child abuse as the focus of concern. That is to say, they have had no support (and often active discouragement) for involvement in less acute preventative work, especially of a long term nature. It is understandable that they have taken colour from their working environment and do not find it easy to shift focus and, in some areas, the attitudes of middle managers may further inhibit change.

This, inevitably, is made more difficult by scepticism, even cynicism, amongst workers and managers about a changed emphasis which does not bring with it increased resources. Deeply scarred by public criticism when they have failed to protect children, it is small wonder that they ask who will defend them if shrinking resources are diverted from child protection to preventative work and tragedy ensues. These fears may result in part from a misunderstanding of what is expected of them. Nonetheless, they are baldly described here to highlight a source of current tension between health and social services professionals. The category of neglect will probably throw up most of the cases which should move between 'in need' and 'protection' provision; thus the approach of the workers to flexible use of the law becomes very important. However, there are a group of neglectful families which fall, fairly and squarely, into 'protection' provision for substantial periods of time. They may benefit from some similar provision offered to less seriously neglected children in need, but this will need to be accompanied by more extensive and precise safeguards.

From an interprofessional perspective, we are at a delicate, yet promising, stage of development. Can we find a way of working together along a continuum of 'prevention'? The introduction of mandatory children's service plans, which themselves necessitate interagency and interprofessional activity, is positive in three respects. First, it endorses a model of working which has in many areas been pioneered by Area Child Protection Committees and thus gives wider legitimacy and status to interprofessional co-operation. Second, such plans take as their starting point the focus on children in need, as defined in the *Children's Planning Guidance* (HMSO 1996). That is to say, there is a concentration upon groups of children who are, in one way or another, more vulnerable than others. It is, therefore, possible (and highly desirable), to raise the profile of 'neglect' as an issue which requires particular attention in relation to interagency co-operation. Third, it seems likely that Area Child Protection Committees will fit well within the structures developed for the delivery of childen's service plans as a whole. Thus the interaction between 'need' and 'protection' services, across agencies, which is crucial in working with neglectful families, will be facilitated.

There are, then, grounds for some optimism that interprofessional work in cases of neglect can become more effective. There is a consensus between agencies that it is an important issue and there is a will to move forward; structures which can facilitate this work exist and are in process of development.

However, there is general agreement amongst key professionals that neglect has not been handled well. Indeed there is a strong sense of unease about it. These impressions were confirmed at two seminars on neglect held in May and June 1997 at Oxford and Nottingham, which were attended by 40 professionals comprising all the central disciplines concerned with child protection, except for the police, but including lawyers. There was a high level of agreement first, that, despite the definitional and conceptual difficulties, the problem of 'thresholds' and the many different facets of the neglect, there was a particular, recognisable group of 'neglectful' families who shared similar characteristics and were distinguishable from others living in similar areas. Second, the overlap and interaction between neglect and emotional abuse was clear. Third, there was concern and perplexity about the construction of *workable* tools for ongoing assessment of the family situation. Fourth, and perhaps most important, there was an acceptance that some of the children in these families were grossly lacking in the basic necessities for healthy development.

However, the degree of consensus between the expert and experienced individuals who took part in these seminars, but who were not asked to discuss the specifics of cases, needs to be considered alongside the views of the wide range and substantial numbers of practitioners who took part in Birchall and Hallett's (1995) research. This revealed variations in the assessment of specific cases, presented as vignettes to them. It was modelled on the pioneering work of Giavannoni and Becarra (1979) who used the technique to explore variations in workers' ratings of diverse incidents. In their vignettes, Birchall and Hallett set out to investigate 'whether professionals report similar views of the severity of the same incident' (p. 118). They used 23 vignettes to elicit views on four categories of abuse: sexual, physical, emotional and neglect. Respondents were asked to assume the child in question was 5 years old; this was 'to maximise the salience' of health visitors and teachers. There were nine vignettes specifically concerning neglect, used in a fairly wide sense to include omission of care and failure to protect the child. The conclusions drawn are as follows:

'Physical and sexual abuse are evidently rated more severely than the other categories by all the professions. Within (all) the categories, it is clearly more difficult to establish either internal or interprofessional consensus about cases less severe. This must cause problems in establishing a baseline for protective intervention. As was expected, cases of neglect and emotional abuse cause most dissensus. Of cases generally, there is total interprofessional consensus in only a minority of cases but there are many areas of agreement within and between the professionals which should support a considerable degree of concensual action.'

(p. 138)

Although the statistics indicate that there is most disagreement between professionals concerning neglect and emotional abuse, this is not as striking as might have been anticipated. Furthermore, the statistical average may mask wide variation between individuals within these groups. Paediatricians, as a group, are near or below the average of other groups but their individual scores vary quite widely; the authors suggest that 'this would simply indicate that the dispute is about per-sonal values rather than professional ideologies' (p. 135).

Thus, the homogeneity which the statistics suggest may be an artefact of the process. Unfortunately, for our purposes, the authors do not indicate whether these individual differences were more evident in some groups or in some categories than others. However, at each end of the 'severity ratings' across all categories of abuse, the health visitors rank the highest and the social workers the lowest, which gives a clear indication of a difference between these groups, even taking into account individual variations. It should be noted that these results do not accord with those of Fox and Dingwall (1988), who found no significant disagreements between these two groups. The possible reasons for this cannot be explored here; the two studies were metho-dologically very different. In focusing upon the Birchall and Hallett's work, I have been influenced by their large sample (over 300 respon-dents), by the very detailed analysis undertaken on the responses and because the data are more recent.

Health visitors and social workers

Birchall and Hallett point out that their findings suggest a high level of anxiety in health visitors. It also appears that social workers are in some important way 'out of step' with many of their colleagues, especially in less serious cases. They found that health visitors (with school nurses) 'stood out from all the rest as easy to co-operate with' (p. 218); they were deemed as 'essential' or important to child protection by 90% of respondents. Yet, of the 'front line' respondents, only about one third felt clear about the role of health visitors. Hallett (1995) comments that both health visitors and their managers stressed 'health promotion' and 'expressed a keen wish not to be involved inappropriately in offering support to families whose primary needs were for material assistance and social work support' (p. 328). However, the knowledge which we have about the characteristics and health problems of neglectful families suggests that health visitors will always be much needed in those aspects of child protection.

It seems, then, that health visitors are in a position of considerable role strain, yet are highly valued by other workers. They are at the front line in the welfare of young children, yet they may perceive themselves, or be perceived, as carrying less status and power than their medical colleagues. In primary health care teams their expertise is not always adequately respected by their 'team leader', the general practitioner. Although, in the vignettes, particular anxiety about neglect rather than other kinds of abuse was not strikingly evident in the ratings, obser-vation and experience suggest that in day to day practice this is very likely to be the case. In cases of sexual and physical abuse, others may be expected to intervene, where possible, more decisively; whereas the health visitor may remain at the forefront, for months or years, in cases of neglect. She will be aware of the 'threshold' problems, of social services' uncertainty about requesting the courts to intervene and of the damage being done, but may feel impotent to effect change. It is hardly surprising that many health visitors welcome the refocusing initiative in principle as offering opportunities to work more constructively with these children and families in need where serious physical and sexual abuse may not be the primary focus.

Why are social workers at the lowest end of the 'severity ratings' in all categories, including neglect? It has been suggested (Dingwall *et al.* 1983; 1995) that social workers may have lower standards of child rearing, in relation to the families with whom they work, than other families in comparable circumstances. However, other factors may account for the findings in the Birchall and Hallett study. First, as I have suggested elsewhere (Stevenson 1996), the wave of pessimism concerning the outcomes for children who are 'looked after' by the system, especially in relation to residential care, is bound to affect the way family difficulties are perceived. Social workers know the dangers and limitations of substitute care better than others and there may be a mental process which results in the 'talking down' of family problems. (Although, in fairness, there was a general consensus across the professional groups on the *most* severe of the case vignettes.) This is particularly likely to be seen in cases of neglect when there is no sharp, defining incident or clear threshold.

Second, and also of particular relevance to neglect, is the problem of cultural relativism, which was discussed more fully in Chapter 4. The term is by no means restricted to the values of people from different ethnic groups. It is also applicable to different social classes and even to different regions within the country. Once sociological eyes have been opened and social workers made aware of the cultural diversity of behaviour, this can lead to excessive reluctance to pass judgement on the child rearing practices of others and, unfortunately, to attribute to cultural factors what is in fact individual and idiosyncratic behaviour. The socialisation, through education and employment, of social workers makes it likely that this tendency will be more apparent in their profession than others. Thus, particularly in response to 'vignettes' on which they have little detail of cases and no responsibility for action, social workers' caution in rating problems severely is not surprising. In neglect, therefore, the evident uncertainty about 'thresholds' is increased by insecurity concerning what constitutes 'normality' in other cultural groups or classes.

Birchall and Hallett (1995) point out that the most numerous disagreements on the vignettes are between social workers and health visitors and that this suggests 'real tensions' between them. It would be interesting to know whether disagreements occurred more in cases of neglect. It seems probable that the tension and anxiety experienced by health visitors over cases of neglect are increased because of social workers' hesitation over such cases. Yet, they are in the front line of communication and co-operation over neglect.

There are three other groups whose position in relation to neglect is crucial. Two of these, general practitioners and paediatricians, have an essential part to play in the health input which is of particular relevance to the topic.

General practitioners

The position of general practitioners in the child protection system has long been considered unsatisfactory by the other participants (Hallett & Stevenson 1980) and is confirmed as remaining so in the studies discussed above. There are complex difficulties underlying this and we have not been successful in addressing these in over 20 years. GP's 'severity ratings' in Birchall and Hallett (1995) were not strikingly different from other professional colleagues, although they tended to be at the lower end of the scale. They did not see neglect differently from other forms of abuse in terms of severity. However, in a questionnaire administered to a large sample, Birchall and Hallett found 'there is a lot of dissatisfaction around general practitioners' role'... Few found them very easy to work with – especially social workers and police. 'Two thirds of paediatricians and health visitors think they perform poorly' (in the field of child protection) (Birchall & Hallett 1995, p. 237).

Hallett concludes, on the basis of both studies, that 'the mandate to work together is not widely accepted by general practitioners, who may have the status and independence to ignore it'. She suggests that they may in fact have 'little to contribute' (p. 333) but points out that 90% of those interviewed considered the GP's role to be 'essential' or 'important' in child protection and that there are striking exceptions to these criticisms. We have understood for a long time (Hallett and Stevenson 1980) that general practitioners, amongst some other professionals, may feel themselves on the 'outer circle' of child protection, seeing very few cases and without a clear role in ongoing work. However, it is important that these problems in establishing the general practitioner within the child protection network should be resolved if the issue of neglect is to be tackled more effectively and systematically. Their importance rests not only on the occasions when clinical judgement needs to be exercised but also as leader of the primary health care team. Such leadership may be of particular importance in cases of neglect. For, in such cases, there are sometimes complicating medical problems in the children; the interaction of these with lack of effective parental care is often highly problematic Yet, as noted above, two thirds of the health visitors are unhappy with their relationships with the general practitioners. (A perception not shared in reverse. GPs were much more content with their HVs!) It is to be hoped that in the revised, forthcoming, *Working Together* (Department of Health 1989), this long-standing national nettle will be grasped. It is apparent that local goodwill and pragmatism are not enough to ensure reasonably adequate and comprehensive involvement of these key players.

Paediatricians

The third group who are of great significance to the handling of neglect cases are the paediatricians. As we have earlier noted, Birchall and Hallett (1995) found their severity ratings were in the median range (though rather low), but pointed out that this might disguise wide individual variations. However, whatever their differences of view about particular situations, a large majority of other professionals regard their role as 'essential' or 'important' but are less happy about working relationships with them. There is a wide spread of views about this from 'very easy' to 'very difficult' which accords well with general anecdotage! It was also clear from Hallett's (1995) study that other workers had less experience of, and were less clear about, the role of paediatricians than they were about some other groups, perhaps reflecting uncertainty about differences in the work undertaken by hospital and community paediatricians and differing views of their role within the latter. However, Hallett also found that, in general, paediatricians were well rated by others in their performance of their role (see Hallett 1995, Table 1 11.9, p. 319).

These findings are less striking than some others but, in view of paediatricians' central position in the assessment of neglect and the advice which they can give both in conferences and outside to other professionals, their role, actual, perceived and potential, would merit further examination, to ensure that their contribution is fully utilised. Paediatricians may hold the 'wild card' in situations such as conferences when crucial decisions are taken Their professional status then becomes very important. Particularly in cases of failure to thrive, sometimes, though not always, associated with neglect, their input to multi-agency working can be highly significant.

The teachers

The fourth group of those who should be centrally involved are teachers, who were respondents in both the studies which we have been discussing. However, it is better to think of school staff as a whole rather than just the teachers. These studies and other observations suggest, for example, that in some areas the school nurse may play a more important part than has been commonly realised. The potential role of education welfare officers, especially in those cases of neglect which involve poor school attendance, is obvious, although there is little recent research to illuminate what part they are actually playing. In general, there has been little discussion in the literature about the role of the school in cases of neglect. Instead, even in such publications as Maher (1987) on the educational perspective in abuse, there was no reference to an educational welfare officer and little to the part played inside the school (as distinct from attendance at conferences) in individual cases of neglect. It is probably generally accepted that the concern of teachers about sexual and physical abuse has been more explicit, especially in relation to anxiety about the impact of formal referral on their pupils. Yet, in discussion, it often emerges that teachers are deeply worried about neglected children and, in primary schools especially, there are often moving accounts of the efforts which they have made to supplement poor care at home by 'unofficial' help about cleanliness and hygiene.

An earlier chapter (6) has discussed the grave and long term effects of neglect on educational attainment. The increasingly competitive emphasis in school on tests and results, the judgements made about schools on the basis of this and severe resource constraints clearly work against the creation of a climate in which damaged children can be nurtured and stimulated intellectually. It will be sad if political emphasis on improving standards and on reducing 'social exclusion' results in neglect of the very children who will not improve without very special attention. It is appreciated that many of these matters are not within the control of the schools and the teachers in them. Their involvement in child protection systems has been complicated by the devolution of responsibility from local education authorities to local governors, with the associated problems of prioritising expenditure. The task of local education departments in co-ordinating child protection arrangements has also been made much more difficult by these arrangements.

It is against this background, therefore, that we examine the findings on teachers of the research conducted in the early 1990s. In the vignettes, Birchall and Hallett (1995) found that the teachers' ratings of abuse generally, with health visitors, were the most severe. 'Teachers and health visitors were markedly different' (p. 134) from the other three groups. Paradoxically, however, 'teachers respond strongly to the vignettes but appear generally distanced from the world of child protection' (p. 136). In the vignettes, difference of opinion between categories of abuse is unclear. It has more to do with the specific aspects of abuse given in the vignettes than with the categories *per se*. Thus, there is no indication that teachers respond more to neglect than sexual, physical or emotional abuse, although in general their ratings are more severe.

Both studies show clearly that the position of teachers is ambiguous. Like general practitioners, they are firmly in the 'outer circle'. 'A worrying number' of teachers are unclear about social workers' roles (Birchall & Hallett 1995, p. 240). 'Teachers were 'five times as likely ... as social workers or the police to give 'don't know' responses and were three times as likely to give no reply' (p. 244). 'The minimal involvement of teachers remains evident even when only head teachers ... (who are said to hold the reins quite tightly) are examined' (pp. 245–6). However, Hallett (1995) (with Gibbons *et al.* 1993) found that teachers were a key source of referrals, and with the health visitors 'were the agency most likely to be involved along with the social services department in ongoing intervention with the child following registration' (p. 333). Hallett commented that although the teachers' role in child protection was valued by others, there was considerable variation in the extent to which they were familiar with procedures and secure in their role. She concluded:

'It may be necessary to spell out more clearly the teachers' role ... Given their key role, efforts need to continue to be directed to raising the levels of awareness and of knowledge about how to respond.'

(p. 334)

In cases of neglect, the educational services have a critical role to play, as much in ongoing monitoring and intervention as in referral. If this is not recognised in general plans for improvement, a small but needy group of children will be further disadvantaged.

The foregoing analysis, then, has focused on five professional groups: general practitioners, health visitors, paediatricians, social workers and teachers (with others in the school). Others, of course, may play a significant part according to the nature of the case, for example, psychologists, clinical or educational. Psychologists have been of particular value in cases when learning disability is a factor. But these five groups (depending on the age of the children) are at the heart of effective assessment and intervention.

Four groups of health professionals cluster around neglect. When the ongoing health of the children is central to the case and especially when there are a number of children in the family, there is a case for a designated 'co-ordinator' of health information, which would emphasise the centrality of the nursing and medical input to neglect. The primary health care team may be in a unique position to undertake this, not least because neglect, as The Bridge Consultancy (1995) point out in the case of 'Paul', is often associated with frequent missed appointments for different children at different outpatient clinics with different doctors in attendance. However, it matters not if there are, locally, different arrangements. The important issue is that a *person* takes responsibility for collating health information and feeding it into other kinds of information from other sources. We have now seen tragic examples of a failure to achieve effective interagency communication, which is a precursor to effective co-operative activity. Whilst not all cases paint such a complex picture of interagency involvement as that of 'Paul', it is salutary to study The Bridge Consultancy (1995) diagram of the network surrounding 'Paul's' family (Fig. 7.1). It will be noted that no fewer than 13 health professionals and agencies are involved.

Three groups of professionals whose views and attitudes require further consideration are first police, second, lawyers, magistrates and judges and third, adult mental health services.

Police

The police were the sixth group in the Birchall and Hallett studies. They were not strikingly out of line with the others surveyed, although in the neglect vignettes they were below the overall average rating of severity in eight of the nine. (The exception described a scenario in which the parents 'never cleaned up'.) The authors further commented, in relation to emotional abuse, that

> 'it is not surprising and may be of little consequence that the police appear less attuned to emotional abuse... They would be unlikely to be concerned in direct investigation of most such cases or to come into conflict over their management.'

(pp. 136–7)

Whilst this is obviously correct, the findings merit some further reflection. In the vignette which the police rated more highly than others, we see a traditional view of neglect as being primarily about dirt. We are familiar with descriptions given in court of such households. This reflects the circumstances in which police often become involved. However, police may be called to homes for the more tangible 'incident-based' events; even when these are not substantiated or sufficiently serious to take action, it is important for the level of awareness of neglect as a wider concept than 'low hygiene' to be raised. Such families are often well known in the neighbourhood and police may have much more useful information to share (often derived from acquaintance with juvenile offenders) than a simplistic and limited 'incident investigation'. Indeed, they may have more of a role in intervention than first appears. There has been a worrying split in our thinking between the juvenile 'victims' and juvenile 'villains' which fails to connect the indications of lack of care and control at home (an aspect of neglect) with some youthful tyrants who dominate the streets or their 'hangers-on'.

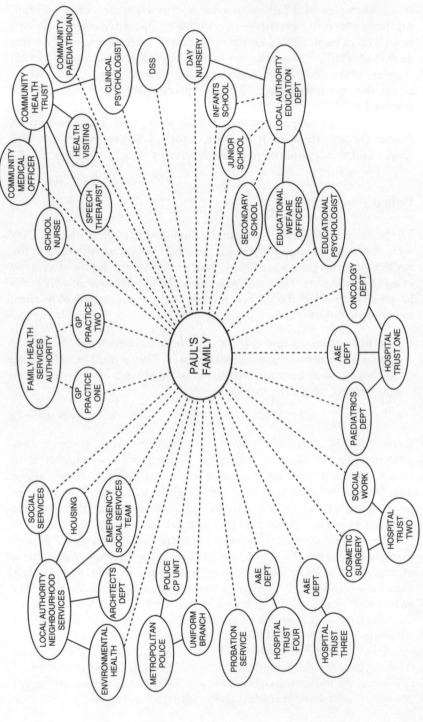

Fig. 7.1 The network surrounding Paul's family (The Bridge Consultancy 1995).

Lawyers, magistrates and judges

In Chapter 1, it was suggested that the failure to delineate the category
of neglect with more precision and firmness, in terms of evidence and
thresholds, may have adversely affected the relationship between the
courts and social services departments. Certainly, the perceptions of
social workers and some other professionals is that they have a much
steeper mountain to climb in order to prove neglect than (for example)
physical injury. This turns, of course, on the nature of the evidence
required; it has been argued that these difficulties are not insurmoun-
table, although the evidence may be of a different kind. To what extent
the fears and anxieties expressed by workers (including some *guardians
ad litem*) that their evidence will be rejected are justified through
experience is not clear. I am not aware of any British research on this
point. One complaint which appears to have some validity is that the
position may be made more difficult because of the stance taken by the
lawyers employed by the local authority, for whom 'winning the case'
may be more important than taking serious concerns to court to share
responsibility. Yet this again turns on the nature of the evidence which
the local authority lawyers perceive as relevant. If this criticism is justified, lawyers must be included in the general reappraisal and better
understanding of 'neglect', as an administrative category of maltreatment.

There are four elements in the judicial process which may give rise to
difficulty. First, there is the need to agree what the parameters for the
assessment of neglect are to be. Crucially, do lawyers, magistrates,
judges and child protection workers have a common basis of understanding of the necessary conditions for healthy development and
conversely, of the serious and long lasting effects on children when
these conditions are not fulfilled?

The evidence that magistrates have access to admirable discussion
and clarification of these issues is to be found in The Magistrates
Association publication (1994) *The welfare of the child; assessing
evidence in children's cases*, a training manual which conveys excel-
lently the essential elements in child development, including attachment
theory, which have to be taken into account in assessing children's
welfare. In the fourth workbook of this publication, Ball and Berkley-
Hill use the definition of neglect from *Working Together* (Department
of Health 1989). They comment:

> 'Neglect is a difficult area in which to assess long-term effects, pos-
> sibly because of the ease with which some surface features are
> superficially put right – for example, the child who is regularly fed
> and bathed while in foster care can look as if he or she has made a
> remarkable recovery. But the real impact of neglect should not be
> viewed lightly and it must be remembered that there are forms of

neglect which do not have obvious physical signs – for example, neglect of a child's emotional needs. Indeed, in discussing neglect, it is virtually impossible to differentiate between physical and emotional needs. Neglect may take many forms – from a lack of care for the physical needs of warmth, safety and nourishment, through a failure to provide consistent love and care, to overt hostility and rejection.'

(p. 16)

They offer the following indicators:

'Practitioners will be taking factors such as those listed below into account when trying to assess the likelihood of neglect:

- the child's physical state. Is he or she physically clean? Are his/her clothes clean?
- appropriateness of dress. Is the child dressed in an appropriate way for his/her size, the weather conditions, etc.?
- nourishment. Is there evidence that the child is well fed? Are there reports, for example from schools, that the child is abnormally hungry?
- safety and warmth. Is the child kept safe by his or her main carers? Are obvious risk areas such as fire guarded? Are risky situations anticipated (e.g. stairs)? Is he or she kept safe from undesirable others (e.g. is the mother willing to leave the child with someone she knows has abused other children)?
- weight loss and failure to grow and thrive physically and psychologically not due to physical or medical factors.
- medical status. Are the child's medical needs acknowledged and responded to? Are the appointments at clinics kept? Does he or she receive prompt treatment for injuries or illness? Are medically prescribed regimes adhered to?
- psychological development. Are the child's needs for psychological safety and development met? This will include needs for control, stimulation, appropriate physical contact, self-esteem, etc.'

Training is also essential for solicitors acting for children and family division judges, though not for barristers, or for solicitors acting for parents. The question is – how far is there in fact a meeting of minds in the courts? We have no evidence of such day to day practice which would enable us to make a fair appraisal of 'the state of the art' at the present time.

The second element in the judicial process concerns thresholds at which significant harm in cases of neglect is reached. As we have seen from earlier discussion, whilst it may be possible to develop the rather more precise criteria for such decisions, the fact remains that for all concerned, whether the professionals or those in the judicial system, difficult and crucial discussions on thresholds in the end remain a matter of judgement in which opinions may unfortunately differ. This is why an agreed starting point on the relevant factors is essential. It is also an area in which those who must decide need to be aware of the class and cultural bias which they inevitably bring to such discussions. For example, in the Maria Colwell inquiry (DHSS 1974), there was disagreement between the chair and a member (myself) on the importance in an appraisal of parental care, of Maria (aged 6) collecting coal from the local shop in a pram and wheeling it home. (I saw it as a local norm, the chair as a further illustration of the mother's maltreatment.)

If neglect is found to be proven, there remains a third crucial element concerning parental capacity to improve their care of the children. The judiciary and magistrates are unlikely to be better equipped than the workers to form a judgement on this and the views of those who have seen parents over longer periods and in the home situation should sometimes carry more weight. However, in this matter all parties may be caught up to varying degrees in balancing the welfare of children with the legal requirement to work with parents and in particular sympathy with some neglectful parents. Whilst not documented systematically, there seems to be at least anecdotal evidence of occasions in which both parties have contributed to protracted and doomed efforts at rehabilitation, in which vital years of children's development have been lost in the vain hope of improvement in their care.

Finally, if and when the time comes for the children to be removed, the care proposed will be the subject of judicial scrutiny. The most likely area of conflict between the social services and the courts is the matter of continuing contact with parents. This is an issue which goes beyond neglected children to child welfare policy generally and is of the utmost importance. From observation and anecdote, as well as reported cases from the higher courts, it is evident that considerable conflict surrounds such decisions and further research and study are much needed. However, as we shall discuss in the final chapters of this book, models of shared care, with or without court orders, might profitably be developed with those neglectful parents whose parenting capacity seems irreparably damaged but who have established relationships with the children and love to offer them. It is to be hoped that such arrangements can be fostered by the courts.

Adult mental health services

Finally, in this consideration of working together in cases of neglect, reference must be made to the 'missing parties' the adult mental health services (who are rarely represented in Area Child Protection Committees). In child protection generally, there has been growing concern that co-operation between the professionals dealing with adults and those whose remit is child protection is often ineffective. The need to make connections through the communication of information and the making of co-ordinated treatment plans is too obvious to require elaboration but, unfortunately, there is ample evidence that this dimension of co-operation does not work well, either in relation to parents with mental health problems or to those with learning disabilities. There are several factors involved, of which organisational fragmentation, with consequently limited, even blinkered views, of professional roles is probably the most important. Furthermore, if the overarching theoretical framework for understanding is individualistic rather than family centred, organisational divisions which put individuals in the family into separate compartments are not challenged. In the case of psychiatry, adult psychiatrists are more likely to adopt an individualistic model of treatment than are child psychiatrists. This may be further complicated by professional rivalries and by 'misconceived' views in confidentiality. At a conference held in Nottingham in 1996, it was evident further dialogue on this would be welcomed by many community psychiatric nurses who are often in a front line position in work with maltreating (or potentially maltreating) parents. At this conference, however, there was also much anxiety about parents whose mental health problems did not fall into categories recognised by adult psychiatrists as requiring, or amenable to, treatment. Terms such as 'personality disorder' or 'psychopathic tendencies' are dreaded by workers who must cope day by day, because of the implications of hopelessness which they convey.

We have already noted (Chapter 4) that many parents with mild or moderate learning disabilities do not receive any adult services from social service departments. This arises at least in part from the concentration of scarce resources on seriously mentally disabled people. But if, as suggested in Chapter 4, there is a need further to explore the parenting difficulties and limitations which may arise from learning disability and more support were to be offered than is presently the case, it is likely that tensions would surface between workers whose emotional and role identifications are with the adults and those for whom the protection of children is the primary focus. The significance of these problems in relation to cases of neglect needs little elaboration. When one bears in mind that many such parents combine elements both of mental disorder and very limited intellectual ability and that the former may include addiction to alcohol or drugs, the need which child protection workers have for advice and guidance, as well as for effective communication and co-operation with colleagues in adult services, is beyond doubt. It is, of course, easy for such workers to have unrealistic expectations. The bald fact is, for example, that *no-one* may know what to do about the parent with a personality disorder! But the time is overdue for an extension of the philosophy and practice of *Working Together* (Department of Health

1989), so that the present highly unsatisfactory situation can be addressed.

Conclusions

Thus, we may have seen that there are many important matters of continuing concern in interprofessional work on neglect cases. They can be addressed through various mechanisms but all have implications for education and training. There are now substantial groups of experienced trainers who are well versed in developing training initiatives. However, in some of the matters which we have considered here, there is a need for the impetus for change to come first from central government. As has been evident throughout this chapter, the matters to be addressed involve a complex interaction between agency roles and responsibility of those professionals, in which the feelings and perception of problems and attitudes of the individuals play a significant part. In relation to neglect, the following areas are of particular importance:

- Work towards a consensus on how various aspects of neglect are viewed by health visitors and social workers. This is essentially best conducted through education and training. In my view, social workers should move towards health visitors in acknowledging the grave effects of neglect.
- As part of a wider initiative on child protection generally, but with particular reference to neglect and emotional abuse, the role of general practitioners as clinicians and leaders of the primary health care team should be the subject of national guidelines. Training initiatives alone will not suffice.
- The role of the schools in supporting seriously neglected children, with particular reference to the lasting damage caused by educational deficits, should be the subject of debate at national and local levels.
- There should be a co-ordinator of health information in cases of neglect.
- The role of the police in relation to neglect requires further consideration, with particular reference to older, delinquent children in such families.
- There is a pressing need for much more research in relation to cases of neglect on relationships between lawyers, magistrates and judges and child protection workers.
- Relations between adult and children's services are of specific importance in cases of ongoing neglect. Both at national and local levels, there is a need for an open dialogue about these matters.

Chapter 8

So What is to be Done?
Moving forward on assessment

This chapter seeks to draw out the implications of the preceding discussion for practitioners and their managers, especially social workers and health visitors. We have argued that there is sufficient uncontentious knowledge of children's developmental needs, of the harm done when these needs are not met and of the qualities of 'good enough parenting' to form the basis for much improved, systematic assessment in cases of serious neglect.

However, although we can assert from theory and research what children need and what neglected children do not receive, it is evident that in practice we are a long way from utilising such knowledge at field level, where it really counts. To move forward, there needs to be a more precise articulation of the 'deficits' resulting from neglect in particular cases. This is essential, not just when there is the looming prospect of a 'court case' but because purposeful plans for family support require an understanding of the particular aspects of family interaction and child care which are problematic and which need attention. As indicated earlier, I have been acutely aware of the ambivalence (to put it no higher) amongst practitioners concerning the introduction of forms, check lists and so on which would further complicate the 'paper work' to which they are subjected. There are quite a large number of rating scales and check lists, many available from the USA, to aid assessment of children's well-being, of the adequacy of caretaking, of parental well-being and other dimensions (Gaudin 1993). (See Appendices for some examples.) Many of these scales cover common ground, confirming the general impression that there is a corpus of agreed knowledge, although it is noticeable that the most obvious differences lie in the area of material deprivation and household maintenance and the criteria used to measure it. In particular, Polansky's oft quoted childhood level of living scale (Polansky 1981), to be found in Adcock and White's (1985) guide *Good Enough Parenting*, would command little confidence amongst British professionals, who would find 'leaky faucets' (taps) or 'lack of draught insulation' unconvincing proxies for neglect!

These scales and check lists can serve two purposes: they offer both specific indicators, which sharpen observation, and ways of measuring severity. If the latter is the goal, the validity of the measuring techniques is obviously important. Whilst there are sophisticated scientific techniques for so doing and most, though not all, of the scales offered have been tested for reliability, there remains a degree of scepticism amongst many practitioners, not least when the 'indicators' are believed to be too bound up with culturally specific behaviours and knowledge. (The acrimonious debate about the validity of intelligence testing is one such example.) Perhaps at a deeper level, and harder to justify to scientifically orientated colleagues, there is a reluctance to seek to capture 'the truth' through the collection of fragmented information. These reservations, bound up with the general resistance to more paperwork, are important factors to take into account in devising more effective working tools. However, these techniques can be extremely valuable in sharpening the observations made by workers, a prerequisite for effective intervention. As discussed in Chapter 5, there is a pressing need to improve the quality of observation, by front line workers, both of the children and of parent–child interaction. In action research on neglect, currently in progress in Nottinghamshire, use of such 'check lists' proved useful when used as a focus for interprofessional communication. Thus, working through statements like those below may be a useful way of drawing out details of concern.

- There is insufficient food in the house to meet the children's needs for the next twelve hours
- Babies and toddlers are given food which is inappropriate for their age
- The parents appear to feed babies without holding them
- The parents have at best only a dim awareness of their children and needs
- Mother/Father cannot show physical affection to the child/children

Such questions may also, in *aggregate*, bring greater awareness of just how unsatisfactory the present situation is. It seems that the present most pressing need is not for quantitative rating scales as such, the value of which some would in any case question, but for guidance on four critical areas of assessment:

- Precisely *what* is missing in the care of these children?
- *How many* dimensions of children's well-being are in 'jeopardy'? (Using the seven dimensions of *Looking After Children*.)
- *What appear to be the effects of these omissions* on the children's development and behaviour?
- *What makes workers hopeful or unhopeful that the situation can be improved* sufficiently to make good these omissions of carers soon enough for the children's developmental well-being?

Since a great deal of knowledge on these matters is 'out there' waiting to be utilised, why is assessment of neglect generally poor, as seems to be the case? There are a number of interlocking factors. The first derives from the move towards a socio-legal model for practice which, as we have previously discussed, is not adequate for the purpose. The ramifications of this profoundly affect organisational ethos and management style. Most strikingly, it has altered the conduct of supervision. It is widely agreed that, within child protection, the supervision of social workers has become heavily focused on procedural matters, with an emphasis on legal accountability rather than on an examination of the nature of the family problems, the implications for intervention and the exercise of professional judgements. The climate has become fundamentally inhospitable for discussion which seeks to examine the family dynamics and relationships in the round, and to put this in a framework for understanding the problems.

Behind supervision on neglect, of course, lie bigger questions concerning the inadequacy of the knowledge foundations laid in basic training, the lack of advanced training and the gaps in attention to neglect in many staff development programmes. An improvement in the supervisory process will not, itself, be sufficient to offset these deficits. The responsibility for the present situations rests with educationalists, employing agencies, politicians and workers themselves and all will have to play a part in improving practice. It is salutary to remind ourselves that not to utilise available knowledge may be regarded as professionally negligent.

These observations have a bearing on the perceived status and expertise in assessment of social workers in relation to other agencies, especially the courts. One of the most unfortunate consequences of the trends in recent years is that the experience and practice wisdom of many social workers have been devalued, in a climate which has been unsympathetic to social work generally. Examples of poor practice have been cited as evidence of overall failure and, as a profession, social workers have lost confidence in themselves as 'experts' in some dimensions of assessment.

In many serious neglect cases, social workers should be competent to contribute significantly to the understanding of family behaviour and process, as well as to utilise and co-ordinate information from others, both field level practitioners from other disciplines and, on occasion, 'the experts'. In a sense (although social workers may sigh!), neglect cases are the very stuff of social work, combining as they do so many 'external' and 'internal' factors to produce a social problem which society cannot ignore. The objective, therefore, must be to strengthen workers' confidence in their capacity to make well informed judgements.

However, if we were to succeed in creating the conditions in which available knowledge can be better utilised, there remains an important question – how to be sensible and economical in pursuit of necessary information to assess and, where appropriate, intervene. This has to be addressed in the context of current changes in referral systems which offer alternative pathways towards services for children in need or children in need of protection and which have to find ways of moving between the two routes as appropriate. Some authorities have already begun this process, for example, Tameside and Nottinghamshire. These initiatives use the *Looking After Children* dimensions (referred to henceforth as LAC) as the basis for the second stage of assessment and have followed the broad design of those materials, but in a much simplified form (see Appendix IX). Furthermore, work funded by the Department of Health in other authorities is in progress to evaluate the usefulness of the materials for work with families in the community. It seems possible that, if a second stage investigation, using simplified versions of the LAC, reveals areas of particular concern (for example, in a child's behaviour or health problems), the more detailed materials might be used to follow this up, without going into the same detail on other dimensions. If those substantiate concern, that might be an indication for expert advice, at which point it is for those experts to decide what use they wish to make of available rating scales.

It is suggested, then, that a common format for the assessment of neglect, both *between cases* and *over time* in particular cases, would be a significant tool in raising standards. The existence of the LAC materials offers a sound basis for authorities to make progress. This is not to underestimate the work needed (and underway) to make sensible application of them to families in the community whose caretakers may find it difficult to talk about such matters and where numbers of children are involved. Such a tool, however, would be an invaluable means of ensuring, on record, consistency of assessment. The inadequacy of information without focus, scattered across ever burgeoning files in neglect cases, is well known. Its purpose would also offer a guide to particular areas of concern and, hence, targets for action. Occasionally, there would be an immediate purpose – to provide sound evidence for the removal of the children; but even if this is not under consideration at the time, the presence of such well ordered material would be of great value in subsequent court proceedings. It is also a useful way of keeping at bay 'the information' overload which is the bane of social services departments and other agencies.

However, there is always a danger of adopting mechanistically certain modes of gathering information, which should only be used to alert us, and which need to be put in the context of some theoretical framework for understanding. This has been one of the criticisms of the use made of the 'orange book' on assessment (Department of Health 1989) In particular, there is a need to assess in a way which takes account of the dynamic interaction between parents and children; for example, in the existing LAC materials, the record for 'family and social relationships' for a child of 1–2 years does not facilitate perceptive observation of a toddler and mother together which might capture the essence of the relationship.

Earlier in this chapter, reference was made to the four critical areas of assessment in serious neglect. It has been argued that the first three concerning the child's well-being, present and future are not, in theoretical terms, seriously controversial; that the difficulties lie much more in the incorporation of knowledge for use within existing (though changing) structures and processes for the systematic and ongoing assessment of neglect.

The fourth critical area concerned the possibilities of change in parental behaviour in time to help the children sufficiently. This is a thorny and complex matter. In Chapter 2, a way of looking at the neglectful family was put forward which showed the number of interlocking systems which bear on the family. If that is so, the assumption must be that change, for better or for worse, in the care offered to neglected children may be effected through systems both inside and outside the family. The departure or death of a close relative in the wider family; the onset of racial harassment; the arrival of a new class teacher; the allocation of a new dwelling; all these and many other factors have the potential to alter the existing situation. They are, of their nature, unpredictable. Thus, they cannot be taken into account in assessing the possibility of 'likely significant harm'. For practical purposes, therefore, it is the past and present behaviour of parents, usually the mother, which, in neglect cases, will form the basis of decisions about the future safety of our children. Gaudin (1993) points out that most measures of risk have not differentiated neglect from abuse but cites Baird and Neufeldt (1988) as an exception. In their studies, they assessed the likelihood of continued neglect in relation to 550 families referred for neglect over a 12 month period. The factors which they drew out included:

- Caretaker neglected as a child
- Single caretaker at time of referral
- Caretaker history of drug/alcohol abuse
- Age of youngest caretaker at time of referral (i.e. youth)
- Number of children at home (i.e. more)
- Caretaker involved in primarily negative social relationships
- (Low) motivation for change on part of caretaker

This analysis does not throw any light on the effects of intervention. Sadly, however, it will not come as a surprise to British practitioners, who will be able to recollect such families without difficulty.

A depressing picture is painted by Crittenden (1988), who also distinguishes between abusing and neglecting caretakers and finds grounds for much more optimism about the former. She concludes that 'neglecting parents ... have a very poor prognosis for improvement with treatment' (p. 184). There are several reasons for this:

'neglected parents tend to be limited intellectually, to have little concept of what is missing from their approach to child rearing and to be embedded in a social system that is materially and socially impoverished. Most important, they do not believe that others can effectively promote change. Thus, they lack skills, goals, resources and motivation... More than anything, they lack a belief in the efficacy of their own efforts,'

(p. 184)

This is a gloomy picture indeed and it is well supported by evidence. There seem to be three implications to be drawn from such findings. First, it is unhelpful to seriously neglected children to be optimistic about the likelihood of significant change in the behaviour of their caretakers. In particular, one must beware the emotional investment in success and over identification with parents, which has been a feature of such cases. Second, however, the judgement that caretakers will not improve sufficiently and in time does not inexorably lead to the removal of the children, although, on occasion, this will be inevitable. Rather, it may lead us to more realistic plans for the children in various domains of their lives. As Crittenden remarks: 'regardless of the parents' responsiveness to treatment, neglected children need preventative intervention' (p. 184). Third, however, as in all child abuse, there is no predictive tool which can adequately take account of the varying circumstances, life events and differing capacities of individuals to assure a given outcome.

We turn to strategies for intervention in the last chapter. This chapter has emphasised the importance of consistent, ongoing and precise assessment as a precursor for action. There are four key issues.

- In the assessment of neglect, multidisciplinary assessment is indispensable, drawing on the extensive knowledge of child development, normal and abnormal, of a range of professionals. Health professionals are likely to have particular importance.
- Social workers have several roles in assessment: in co-ordinating overall assessment of a family, in integrating consideration of factors external and internal to the nuclear family and in contributing to information about and observation of parent and child behaviour and interaction.
- The objective should be to have an *economical* but *systematic* and *ongoing* system of gathering and recording relevant information when neglect is considered, be it an actual or potential problem which fits into the current review of referral processes and of the LAC materials.
- The existing evidence of the difficulty in achieving change in neglectful parents should be honestly faced so that realistic plans can be made in reasonable time.

Chapter 9
So What is to be Done? Intervention

The last chapter ended on a cautionary note: it is very hard to effect change in the behaviour of seriously neglectful caretakers. Such a conclusion, it is argued, is a necessary jolt to our way of thinking about intervention in such cases. The prevailing and powerful ethos of 'partnership with parents', so strongly endorsed in The Children Act 1989, together with a deep pessimism about the capacity of the system to offer children good enough substitute care, have combined to produce an unsatisfactory situation. Intervention is characterised by bursts of somewhat fragmented activity; there is much underlying anxiety in the professionals concerned, but a difficulty in establishing systematic and purposeful plans to protect the children. At a time when 'family support' and 'prevention' are again on the official political agenda, it is particularly appropriate and important to consider the implications of emerging policy and practice for this particular group of families. The debate about 'prevention' as an objective of social policy for families raises complex questions and controversial issues, much of which is beyond the scope of this book to explore in detail. However, it is important to place the discussion of neglect in the wider context.

Many professionals and Area Child Protection Committees have found it helpful to utilise the medical model of prevention, primary, secondary and tertiary levels. Gough (1993) sums up the three levels, as constructed in medicine, as:

- Primary: interventions aimed at 'whole' populations
- Secondary: interventions aimed at individuals or groups considered to be at risk
- Tertiary: reactive interventions concerned to prevent unwanted events recurring

Whilst there are difficulties and tensions in transferring such a model to the field of social welfare (Parton 1985; Gough 1993), it remains a useful way of distinguishing different kinds of activity within this field. Hardiker and colleagues have explored these issues most helpfully and their work has been utilised by many local authorities and Area Child Protection Committees (Hardiker *et al.* 1991(a); Hardiker *et al.* 1991(b)).

In relation to neglect, we do not develop here the possibilities of primary prevention, for example, by programmes on parenting for school aged young people. Seriously neglectful parents will have needs and difficulties which cannot be forestalled by broadly targeted early interventions of this kind. However, likely future problems in individuals may be identified in the process of providing general programmes. In particular, the identification of and support for people with learning disabilities who may become parents is well worth further consideration. Whilst it has been argued that there is a danger of stigmatising such people by attributing parenting difficulties to the learning disability per se, rather than associated difficulties, it is surely justified to give early attention to young people who may be particularly challenged by the complexities of child rearing.

The main focus of this chapter is upon that level of intervention which might be described as tertiary. Our emphasis throughout has been on serious neglect, which places the children in serious jeopardy. Common sense suggests, of course, that earlier identification and intervention ('secondary intervention') is highly desirable; such cases are on a continuum rather than clearly distinguished. Thus, much of the discussion which follows is applicable to a range of cases which fall at different points on the continuum. Indeed, it would be understandable and in line with present thinking if some neglectful families were to be supported as 'in need' rather than requiring child protection procedures. However, it is not an option to turn away from the gravest cases. The consequences for the children are too damaging.

The implication of the 'ecological map' presented in Chapter 2 is that intervention may be attempted of many kinds and in many ways, related to the various systems which impact on the family. This does not necessarily mean that intervention need or should address so many diverse factors in individual cases. The question to be asked is: 'what might make a difference in this case?'. As Gibbons *et al.* (1990) point out:

> 'there are few controlled evaluated studies of the effectiveness of measures intended to prevent serious parenting problems leading to the break up of families. The scarcity in Britain of controlled evaluation of the effectiveness of measures intended to beat child abuse and neglect is particularly striking.'

> (pp. 22–3)

Gibbons *et al.* further point out that even in the USA, where there is a 'huge descriptive literature' about child abuse, 'there are fewer controlled studies of the effectiveness of intervention (p. 23). Unfortunately, even in one large, multisite, evaluative programme involving 3000 families, 'the research was not well controlled and the outcome measures used were questionable' (p. 23).

However, the significance of the findings of these studies, and others, for intervention in neglect has been well summarised by Gaudin (1993) and, despite overall pessimism, there are some useful indicators of ways to direct efforts more effectively. Gaudin, unsurprisingly, confirms that 'the most powerful predictor of outcome' was the severity of the family's problems and that the presence of alcohol and drug problems 'consistently correlated with less successful outcomes' (p. 35). However, he identifies some particular approaches or methods in which interventions have proved more effective than others. In the discussion which follows, I have broadly adopted the same headings.

Multiservice interventions

Gaudin's view, which would be widely shared in this country, albeit expressed differently, is that the many different problems of neglectful families are likely to require a range of inputs from different agencies and professionals. He points to several examples of projects designed to offer multiservice interventions from which there has been some promising outcomes. However, these are relatively sparse and this may be an area in which British practice is further advanced, partly because of some fundamental differences in the organisation of social provision, including health services. It may also be that the British emphasis on 'working together' in child protection over 20 years enables us to build on these foundations and to explore specific ways of focused collaboration over cases of neglect. As we have seen in Chapter 6, there are formidable difficulties in achieving this, many of which arise from organisational boundaries and bureaucratic rigidity.

However, there would seem to be one area in particular concerning neglect in which progress is urgently required, that is at the interface between health, social services (statutory and voluntary) and education for pre school children). It seems likely that this is best achieved (and there are promising examples and initiatives) through some kind of family centre in which emphasis is placed in these three spheres on the co-ordination of intervention at face to face level. However such projects are developed, and it is acknowledged that the practical difficulties are sometimes formidable, the ideal to be realised is to create a holistic structure which mirrors the holistic needs of the children. To achieve this, the proximity of workers from different disciplines and of parents and children to each other is a powerful stimulus (although it needs purposeful reinforcement) to a spirit of co-operative endeavour and to mutual learning from each other.

Family focused intervention

Daro (1988), who reviewed the demonstration projects referred to earlier, suggested that intervention which included other family members as well as the principal carer was more successful. Such a conclusion is consistent with the need to alter the balance in a dysfunctional family system; that is to say, it is not simply about helping the principal carer: it will involve also the children and whenever possible, of course, other adult figures. Although the discussion in the USA literature appears to focus on the 'nuclear family' in this context, it may well be that there are other kin who are considered crucial to the functioning of that unit and who should be included in a systemic approach to the situation (Chapter 4).

This is a well trodden path for family therapists. Although there are active practitioners in this country and many variants on the theme, this body of theory has had little influence on the mainstream practice of social workers with neglectful families, perhaps because it has been perceived as somewhat esoteric, even elitist. Its value has been questioned for work with families whose commitment to 'talking treatment' is doubtful and who lack insight into their difficulties. Whilst it is unlikely that the traditional techniques of treatment would be applicable to such cases, it would be regrettable if the underlying theory were not incorporated into intervention strategies. Its relevance is seen most sharply in relation to the 'missing men' in the analysis of neglectful families (Chapter 4). Such men, fathers or partners, may be physically 'missing' so far as mothers are concerned, but yet may be highly influential in the family. Or they may be transient figures whose behaviour and attitudes play a highly significant part in family functioning at certain times. Neglect, for example, may be a failure to protect against harm and the presence of a certain man in the home may be a sexual and physical threat to the child. We are dealing with highly unstable systems. Similarly, the build up of destructive interaction between mothers and certain children may require two pronged intervention to modify the behaviours of both. Gaudin (1993) points to the value of this approach in helping to establish clearer 'intergenerational boundaries, clarify communication amongst family members ... and enable parents to assume a strong leadership role in the family' (p. 37).

It seems, therefore, that both in the essential 'message' of the theory (based on ideas of systematic functioning) and in the application of the theory to practice, there are good grounds for refining this way of working in relation to certain neglectful families.

Family preservation services

This phrase refers to particular modes of short term intensive work with families adopted in the USA. An early experiment was 'Homebuilders', 'home based, extremely time limited (days or weeks), goal specific'. 'It featured psychologist directed, interpersonal guidance, plus concrete services' (Kahn & Kammerman 1996).

These experiments, developed in various states of the USA (aided by federal grants), were specifically designed as crisis intervention to avoid family break up. All such programmes, according to Gaudin (1993), shared the following characteristics, although there were variations within those. These are:

- Focusing services upon the entire family
- Providing a range of tangible, supportive and therapeutic services
- *Using short term intervention of six months duration or less* [my italics]
- Establishing small caseloads
- Using well trained, supervised and supported caseworkers

In evaluating the success of such projects, it has to be borne in mind, first, that when the criteria for referral are genuinely restricted to 'last minute crisis intervention', the dice must be loaded against success, second, that strategies for medium and long term intervention are likely to be very important in some cases and that success must not be defined as 'preventing breakdown' without an assessment of the costs to the children of keeping the family intact.

Gaudin, concludes, nonetheless, that this model of intensive short term intervention offers promise generally with abusive and neglectful families, but the evidence suggests that the programmes were less successful with neglectful families than with families at risk from other kinds of maltreatment (p. 38). Nonetheless, he claims 'the overall success is impressive' (p. 38); that is to say, neglect is the most difficult area to work in but, even so, considerable benefits can be obtained from it.

The gains of such programmes for work in Britain with neglectful families might lie in two areas. First, they may be particularly valuable when, within the context of long-standing neglect, there is a particular crisis episode, such as the illness of a mother or child or the desertion by a partner. Second, such involvement with the family is likely to be extremely illuminating. Well used, it would be invaluable for planning future work. Nor is it sensible to reject it on grounds of expense when the costs of family break up are so much higher.

However, such measures should be viewed with the utmost caution lest they create false expectations of 'a quick fix' in an organisational culture which has, in recent years, laid increasing emphasis on any time limited intervention. As we have already demonstrated, the long term needs of neglectful families are considerable. The only sensible strategy would be to use such intensive periods of intervention as part of a longer term plan; phased, rather than abrupt, withdrawal of such sessions should be the norm. If, with these safeguards plans could be put in place for careworkers on occasion to offer intensive home support as part of an overall plan, with clear objectives, effective supervision and support and co-ordinated input from other agencies, there is little doubt it would be helpful in some cases. However, those objectives need to be based in an explicit attempt to understand the underlying nature of the problem: why is neglect occurring and, therefore, what kinds of input are most needed to support adults and children? Plans, however purposeful, which are not adequately connected to the nature of the problem, are ineffective in the longer run, even if temporary improvement is achieved.

Group approaches

The evaluation of the demonstration projects suggests that those which included group methods were more successful than those which did not. For neglectful families, groups that provided

> 'very basic child care, information and skills, problem solving, home management and social interaction skills were more successful with neglectful parents than those offering more general content on child development and needs of children.'

> (Gaudin 1993, p. 38)

However, neglectful parents are likely to be ill at ease in groups; indeed, their attendance is often erratic. Therefore, guidelines for conducting groups for such parents are helpful, such as:

- Structured group activities, particularly at the beginning, are necessary to relieve anxiety and provide direction.
- Refreshments are an important element in 'nurturing' a neglectful parent.
- Groups should be planned to last 3–6 months.

In Britain, Smith and Pugh (1996) surveyed 38 group based parenting programmes and described their characteristics. Neglectful parents and abusive parents are not specifically singled out in their survey but four projects, Newpin (Pound 1994), the Special Parenting Programme (for parents with learning disabilities), Mellow Parenting and Family Nurturing Network have particular relevance to our topic. They are described as designed to serve 'parents with multiple problems and very low self esteem'. These programmes have been the subject of various kinds of evaluation, but Smith and Pugh conclude:

> 'We still do not know enough about which programmes work best for particular parents with their particular set of needs. This is really the key question to which policy makers and practitioners require answers.'

> (p. 39)

They suggest, however, that there are some useful indicators. For example, concerning the Mellow Parenting programmes, they find that the following approach has resulted in significant improvements:

> 'for parents with severe parenting difficulties in the context of social stress and disadvantage, the packaged programme which includes a psychotherapy group to enable (exploration of feelings) ..., shared activities with parents and children, and discussion of parenting topics using video work.'

> (p. 39)

British practitioners will be familiar with other kinds of group techniques designed to improve parental functioning, not included in the Smith and Pugh survey. One such, called Fun with Families, used and evaluated in Nottinghamshire, although not especially directed at neglectful families has findings of much interest for helping them. This model was developed by a Leicester based centre, for use in family centres. 'The Fun with Families programme provides groups of parents with an intensive, 7 week training package designed to help parents whose children are displaying behavioural difficulties such as aggression, defiance, temper tantrums or sleep problems. The main objective of a Fun and Families group is to apply social learning theory to individual child care circumstances. Parents are helped to make clear sense of what their children are doing and why they are doing it. The aim is to give practical, down to earth suggestions to assist them in changing their children's behaviour and allow them to regain parenthood as a 'fun experience' (Charles *et al.* 1996).

The overall findings of the evaluation were good; both workers and parents were very positive. However, a number of the facilitators

> 'expressed doubts as to whether parents would contrive to apply the material and transfer their learning to deal with fresh behavioural problems ... There was a general feeling that the positive changes ... could be extinguished if the material was not reinforced ...'

> (p. 5)

There was also concern that nearly all those attending groups were mothers. This sometimes meant that there were not consistent messages from both parents. However, the increased awareness in the facilitators of the families' problems and in parents of the possibility of behaving more constructively to their children shone through the comments. Facilitators were

> 'shocked by the degree of emotional poverty with which parents were faced ... These parents, who had never been praised as children, found it difficult to identify "good" behaviour or to define their children's positive characteristics.'

> (p. 7)

The eagerness of participants to learn how better to manage their children was palpable and they spoke of enjoyment and fun in the groups, from which they personally gained much.

An important aspect of these groups was that a number were jointly facilitated by health visitors and family centre workers; each brought different strengths and reacted differently to the use of the programme. It would be hard to imagine a more productive way of working together.

The report which deals, inter alia, with training and organisational and management issues demonstrates that the programmes require careful and intensive preparation and that their relative success raises further questions, particularly concerning the ways in which such projects, and the learning from them, can be spread throughout the organisations and personnel involved.

As with other aspects of provision, there are difficult issues concerning the extent to which recruitment for such groups should be 'targeted' on parents who have particular difficulties. There is a strong, understandable desire to avoid, wherever possible, the stigmatising effects of provision which singles out abusive and/or neglectful parents. But this has to be weighed against the needs which some parents may have for a different style of group or for different kinds of advice and help. It is particularly unhelpful if, for example, neglectful parents drop out from groups in which they feel uncomfortable or inadequately supported. There is a pressing need for further exploration of these issues.

Techniques of working with families

Gaudin (1993) briefly discusses the use of a range of techniques involving direct work with family members and points to evidence that these have been found to be effective in working with neglectful families, especially when they are focused on concrete problems 'with clearly defined short range goals and well defined intervention activities' (p. 40). Such methods may be based on principles of 'task focused casework' (Goldberg et al. 1985), familiar to many British workers although sometimes oversimplified and thus distorted. They may be based on behavioural and social skills approaches (Sheldon 1986). Although theoretical origins may differ, successful methods seem to share a concentration on clearly defined goals and structured activities. Gaudin suggests that the use of printed materials, books, charts, etc. has been found to be useful (see McGaw (undated), Chapter 5) and that 'the use of modelling, coaching, rehearsing and feedback' (p. 40) can be particularly helpful in enhancing neglectful parents' social skills. An emphasis on the acquisition of skills is more likely to have an enduring effect than simply the provision of support. Such a finding chimes well with a professional ethos which seeks to build on strengths and on enhancing the self confidence so conspicuously lacking in many of the neglectful families known to the professionals. This way of working has been intuitively understood by workers, especially those based in family centres, and there are many examples of creative and imaginative work along these lines. It is helpful to know that it has proved valuable but it has to be recognised that in seriously neglectful families there is often a constellation of pressing problems and difficulties of which focused interventions on particular issues form only a small part, There is a danger that the achievement of certain limited goals may generate undue optimism in workers about the overall prognosis for change. This is entirely understandable but dangerous. A well co-ordinated intervention plan will ensure that someone is deputed to stand back and assess progress 'in the round'.

A programme designed to improve social skills, and therefore self esteem of neglectful parents, usually mothers, needs to address more than 'family related' and relationship skills. As this book is being written, there is much media attention upon the present Labour government's plans to encourage lone mothers to take employment where possible. Many of the women about whom we are concerned start a very long way back in terms of employability; for example, they lack basic literacy and, increasingly important, simple technological skills. They are likely to be the women who find it particularly difficult to participate in schemes made generally available. Intervention strategies which see such women not only as mothers but also as adult persons with a broad need for social acceptance would be of particular value.

Strengthening informal support networks

In Chapter 4, we pointed out that the existence of 'kith and kin' in the lives of neglectful families has both constructive and destructive potential. Gaudin (1993) describes the research as showing that 'the informal social networks of neglectful parents are typically closed, unstable and tend to be dominated by often critical, non supportive relatives' (p. 48). Therefore, in asking in what ways support networks can be strengthened, effort will need to be directed in two ways. First, in relation to relatives there has to be a realistic understanding of the extent to which, and the ways in which, relatives are already intertwined with the daily life of the family in question. Whilst there may be cases in which there is a total deficit (as when a mother who has been in care has lost contact with her relatives), it is equally or more likely that a neglectful parent will be connected to relatives who have their own histories and problems of deprivation or violence. Those connections may be tight or loose; they are a 'given' in the situation which the workers confront. The workers will need to assess the contribution such relatives may make, for better and for worse, to the family in question and make a judgement as to the ways in which that contribution could be reduced, modified and enhanced. It is important to examine the underlying effects of practical changes of family interaction. Child care is an obvious example. The advantages of arrangements by which children are cared for by relatives – let us suppose by helping with transport – need to be considered in relation, not only to the quality of care of the children, but to the further contact and dependency which this may create between the adults. It is to be hoped that developments in Family Group Conferences, discussed in Chapter 4, will throw new light on the complex dynamics in the wider family network which can be incorporated into family work more generally. There is often a strong sense of powerful individuals who have stayed in the shadows so far as the professionals are concerned. Grandmothers, in particular, have often been significant in making referrals to the authorities; yet their own parenting may have been demonstrably unsatisfactory or unsuccessful. The dynamics of such situations are inevitably complex.

More generally, Gaudin (1993) discusses methods of enhancing network supports outside the family. Amongst other methods, he refers to the use of volunteers and parent aides 'to expand and enrich impoverished resources of networks and provide new information, positive norms and helpful suggestions about child care' (p. 41). He refers specifically to the proven effectiveness of 'paid or volunteer paraprofessionals' in work with neglectful families (p. 41). These findings confirm and strengthen the present British interest on the part which can be played by organisations such as Home-Start. *Children's Service News* (Department of Health 1997) gives an account of a 3 year research study on Home-Start (Frost *et al.* 1997). This describes the evaluation of the CHIPS (Comprehensive Home-Start Initiative for Parental Support) initiative.

Home-Start is a voluntary organisation, staffed by volunteers. These volunteers offer regular support, friendship and practical help to young families under stress in their own homes, helping to prevent crisis and breakdown. (Home-Start: statement of principle). The range of families helped is, of course, much wider than those on which this book is focused and many fall within the category of those we can describe as needing 'secondary' preventative activity. Frost *et al.* found that in 61% of the families studied, parenting difficulties had been identified. One in ten cases had identified child protection concerns; in about three quarters of the families, there were issues relating to the confidence and self esteem of adults, especially mothers (Department of Health 1997). The evaluation research strongly confirms the value of the Home-Start model as seen by the professional 'referrers', usually health visitors and social workers, and by the users, parents and children.

The question which remains to be addressed is whether such a model can be effective in strengthening social support to seriously neglectful families. Frost *et al.* noted that social workers were anxious about referring to volunteers, cases in which there was a strong child protection element. This has been a concern elsewhere where volunteers are used (Pound 1994). As Frost *et al.* pointed out, there are issues, such as confidentiality, which need further discussion and clarification; they may, on occasion, mask deeper uncertainties and sometimes prejudice about the respective roles of professionals and volunteers. However, there are important questions of accountability and clear communication which would have to be carefully examined, were volunteers to be used in the support of these precarious families, where children may be at serious risk. In referring to 'paraprofessionals' as well as volunteers, Gaudin (1993) raises the need for training and supervision in this kind of work. The objectives of the work are in essence simple, but in practice may prove very difficult in the complex family situations which volunteers are likely to encounter. Offering emotional and practical support, child care and shared social activities can be a straightforward, kindly activity or an immensely delicate and complicated process. In particular, where Home-Start volunteers seek to meet children's needs, physical, emotional, social and educational, more directly, they have to be careful not to undermine parental confidence.

There is a longstanding tension, familiar to all who work with volunteers, between, on the one hand, ideals of spontaneity and informality, and on the other, a sufficient measure of training and support to ensure that difficult human situations are sensitively handled. As one moves along the continuum of families requiring the type of help which Home-Start (and other comparable organisations) offers towards the cases of serious neglect, it becomes less feasible to depend solely on 'the milk of human kindness' – although a good deal of that is required! It remains to be seen whether the model is appropriate for this focused and intensive work, but it provides an excellent opportunity to experiment with ways of relieving the social isolation and associated problems which have been found to be characteristic of neglectful families. Frost *et al.* (1997) described the role of Home-Start workers as 'negotiated friendship' and stressed that it can be a form of 'intermediate support'; that is to say, the phrase is 'an attempt to express the gap between formal and informal support (Department of Health 1997). Of its general value, in preventative strategies, there can be no doubt; the unaffected warmth which is characteristic of the participants is contemporary proof that altruism, as a social value, is alive and well.

Direct services for neglected children

Thus far, our discussion has focused on interventions which have been primarily, though not exclusively, about the adults within neglectful families. However, if we are realistic about the difficulties and likely limitations in achieving behavioural change sufficient for children's safety and healthy development, a key aspect of intervention must be concerned with services to children directly. The rest of this chapter centres on this theme.

Gaudin (1993) comments that most of the intervention programmes reviewed in the USA have focused services on parents and that 'few offer direct therapeutic services to the children'. However, those which attempted to remedy directly the effects of neglect showed promising results: 70% of the children served in this way showed improvements in all areas of functioning. 'Therapeutic day care services for pre school children proved to be the most effective service for both the neglected and the physically abused children' (p. 41).

For children who are already suffering grave consequences of the deficits within their home environment, it would seem that the highest priority in intervention should be the flexible provision of supplementary care. This supplementary care can take many forms, of which the following are examples. (There can be 'variations on the theme' to suit particular circumstances, parents and children, taking into account whether the 'deficits' are pervasive or in particular developmental domains.)

A continuum of care

- Care, play and activity which is home based through the provision of volunteers/paraprofessionals.
- For preschool children, regular daily care through nursery/pre school provision in semiformal surroundings, such as family centres.
- For preschool children, regular daily care through the use of childminders (Department of Health 1997).
- For school aged children, some provision of daily care which extends beyond ordinary school hours, probably through a form of 'daily fostering' or group arrangement. (In Israel, where the school day ends at lunchtime, there are in place some arrangements to care for some children outside the home for quite long periods in the day.)
- For children of all ages, although less desirable for very young children, a range of planned, regular 'breaks' away from home. This is the equivalent to 'respite care' used for disabled children and their families.
- Older children may spend part of the week, or month or year with another family or in residential facilities.

Each one of these raises difficulties. It is not easy to find the right people to provide the care. There are bureaucratic obstacles; it requires very sensitive handling with regard to the feelings of all concerned; such plans involve expenditure. But we have to ask – is there another way? Removing children is a dangerous last resort and very expensive; changing the quality of home care sufficiently is often not possible. Leaving children in fundamentally unsatisfactory environments is morally unacceptable and dangerous to future generations. Is it beyond the capacity of administrators and practitioners to devise mechanisms for flexible 'packages' which utilise, but expand and modify, the many excellent schemes which presently exist in various localities but which are fragmented and partial, often depending too heavily on the good will, imagination and energy of individuals.

These issues have been given added impetus by the present 'refocusing initiative', although their application to the issue of neglectful families needs more detailed consideration. Aldgate *et al.* (1996), for example, provide a valuable analysis of the potential of 'respite accommodation' under the provisions of The Children Act 1989, for a wider range of needy children. They point out that its use must be consistent with the concept of partnership with parents and that parents should be 'expected and enabled to retain their responsibility' (Department of Health 1989, p. 2).

In 13 areas which they studied, Aldgate *et al.* (1996) found that 'effective respite accommodation was being offered by social service departments and voluntary agencies to a wide range of families under stress' (p. 150) of various kinds, not only where there was a disabled carer. They then followed 60 families through a period of respite accommodation.

> 'At the beginning of the study, parents were experiencing problems related to income, housing, health, and the care and day-to-day management of their children. They also felt unconfident about their parenting skills, had low self esteem and little support from families and friends. By the end of the study, parental self esteem had improved, as measured on a standard test. As importantly, parents felt more in control of their lives, their preoccupation with their own chronic health problems had shifted and they had a more realistic view of their abilities and lives. Over half the parents began to address their social isolation by the end of the study. Around one third of the parents commented on the fact that establishing links with carers helped them feel more part of the community.'
>
> (p. 150)

It is evident from the description of these families that a good many of their characteristics were those which we have seen in neglectful parents. However, it may well be that the intensity of some difficulties and some additional problems, particular to such parents, would further complicate the task of arranging and managing short term placements for such families. The children's need for them, however, may be equally, or more, pressing.

Aldgate *et al.* outline the purposes for which respite care is appropriate:

'• To provide relief from the normal stresses of being a parent
• To provide children with relief from stressful family living
• To help manage children's behaviour
• To provide a link with the community for families living in social isolation
• To help with relief from the stress of living in continuing poverty
• To offer an alternative to admission to full time accommodation
• To provide a relief for sick parents
• To provide an early diversion from potential physical abuse
• To build parents' self esteem
• To offer a different and relaxing experience for children'

(p.151)

Many of the opportunities which this list suggests are obviously relevant to the support of neglected children as well as their parents. Indeed, one might develop and expand the possible gains to neglected children, as individuals, of reliable periods of 'good enough' care, in all aspects of their development, not least the physical. Experience of arranging such placements, for whatever purposes, has shown that intimate and sensitive feelings are aroused both in all the adults involved and in the children. The more inadequate and/or guilty the parents feel, the more difficult it may be to manage the placements constructively. Aldgate *et al.* point out the importance of the social worker, not only as 'direct service provider' but as an 'enabler, who helps adults and children reflect upon the experience and learn from it' (p. 150).

The results of the placements studied by Aldgate *et al.* are highly relevant to our theme. For example, parental self esteem improved and over half the parents began to address their social isolation. The emphasis of the service was on providing a family placement that did not threaten parental responsibility. The children who were observed and talked to were between 1 and 15 years. They were 'usually quite clear what the arrangements were and why they had been made' and were very positive about the experience. Furthermore, of the 60 families offered such respite care, only two entered permanent care. However, Robinson (1996), in a review of short term care, points out that this conflicts with evidence from the USA. More research is needed on this. Nonetheless, in the cases we are here considering, once it has been decided that circumstances at home are simply not 'good enough', an intervention which eventually leads to placement may be the only realistic alternative.

Overall, therefore, there is every reason to pursue such initiatives in relation to seriously neglected children, although it is clear that they will present some of the most challenging 'partnerships' for all concerned. Aldgate *et al.* (1996) give a number of helpful examples of the steps which need to be taken in making such arrangements. Many of these would apply equally well to the range of 'supplementary care' plans suggested here: they can best be summed up as steps which demonstrate awareness of, and sensitivity to, the ambivalence which is inherent in situations of shared care in all its variants.

The spirit and intention of The Children Act 1989, and the present emphasis on family support, clearly expect that arrangements such as those described above will be made by voluntary agreement between the parties. Realistically, although this is not comfortable to acknowledge, sometimes neglectful parents have to be made aware that the present care of the children is unacceptable and some alternative plans have to be made. There will be times when refusal to co-operate is the signal that the end of the road has been reached and that there is no alternative but to seek an order for the children to be cared for away from home. More difficult still, there will be times when apparent compliance masks a rejection of the arrangements or, at the least, of extreme ambivalence which ensures that plans go wrong! Children, of course, are much less likely to settle in these circumstances. On occasion, such evidence may be needed to demonstrate that there is no real will to achieve partnership in improving the care of the children.

Robinson (1996) points out that short term care for children raises a number of important policy issues, of which

'inequalities relating to host carers in family based services need to be removed; at present there is no consistency in payment made to link families or befrienders... Offering a reasonable income may encourage some members of the community to be carers who could not otherwise afford to come forward. This may make it possible to link greater numbers of families on low incomes with carers in similar circumstances.'

(p. 264)

Robinson concludes that

'the research indicates that community based developments which do not pathologise the children and families that use them offer hope for reducing social isolation and strengthening family unity.'

(p. 265)

Conclusions

In this chapter, we have seen that there is some energetic, committed work taking place in this country which bears on neglect, even if not targeted solely at it. This work in general shows that, where evaluations have been done, including the work described by Aldgate *et al.* the help received has been much valued by parents and children and resulted in at least short term improvement. How do we progress? There are six key issues:

- Helping seriously neglectful parents and their children is, par excellence, an interprofessional activity and demands focused co-operation, especially between health visitors, social workers and teachers.
- Intervention plans have to be derived from more effective assessment based on both the general situation and specific areas of difficulty which can be addressed.
- There are a wide range of theories and methods of family social work upon which to draw; there is some cumulative evidence, unsurprisingly, that a style of work which is direct and very focused pays off best, but such interventions need to be accompanied by a careful overview of the total family situation. Parental groups offer particular promise.
- A systemic approach involving the wider family is worthy of further exploration.
- There is room for much further exploration of the role of volunteers or paraprofessionals, such as family aides with seriously neglectful families. In particular, we need to know more about the impact of such help when offered for either short term emergencies only or for long periods.
- Because of the available evidence on the difficulties of altering parental behaviour, strategies for direct help to children should be at the forefront of intervention, with flexible plans for 'shared care'.

Postscript

We have come full circle and it is time to acknowledge again, as at the beginning of this book, that there are problems, which loom over neglectful families and their workers, of poverty and of serious resource constraints. No themes developed here are intended to distract attention from the intolerable material hardship in which most neglectful families live and the near intolerable resource shortages which beset many who work with them. However, I hope that the analysis presented here will offer stimulation and encouragement to think freshly about the families in every part of the country who 'bump along the bottom' with disastrous consequences for the children.

There seem to be three requisites for this to happen. First, we can utilise existing knowledge more efficiently for assessment. Second, we must build on good foundations of interdisciplinary practice; third, organisational barriers to innovatory practice can be lowered so that imagination and creativity can be freed even in conditions of scarcity.

Appendixes

Appendix I

About Parent–Child Interactions: Event Recording

Visit No: Assessor: Name of client:

	often	seldom	almost never
Child's reactive and proactive behaviour:			
1 Playing family			
2 Laughing/smiling			
3 Running			
4 Talking freely			
5 Coming for help			
6 Coming for comfort			
7 Cuddling up to parents			
8 Responding to affection			
9 Responding to attention			
10 At ease when parents are near			
11 Joining in activities with other children			
12 Not frightened when approached by parents or corrected			
Father's/mother's reactive and proactive behaviour:	often	seldom	almost never
1 Talking to the child			
2 Looking at the child			
3 Smiling at the child			
4 Making eye contact (lovingly)			
5 Touching (gently)			
6 Holding (closely, lovingly)			
7 Playing			
8 Cuddling			

	often	seldom	almost never
9 Kissing			
10 Sitting the child on the lap			
11 Handling the child in a gentle way			
12 Giving requests (as opposed to commands)			
13 Helping the child if it is in difficulties			
14 Encouraging the child when it cries or when it is hurt			
15 Being concerned about the child			
16 Picking the child up when it cries or when it is hurt			
17 Answering the child's questions			
18 Not ignoring the child's presence			
19 Emotionally treating the child the same as other children			
20 Handling the children consistently			
Siblings' reactive and proactive behaviour:			
1 Playing with the child			
2 Talking to the child			
3 Participating in activities			
4 Accepting the child			
5 Treating the child well			
6 Pushing the child away and rejecting it			
7 Blaming the child for everything that happens			
8 Protecting the child			
9 Helping the child when in difficulties or in trouble			
10 Scapegoating the child			

From Iwaniec, D. (1995) *The Emotionally Abused and Neglected Child* (p. 91). John Wiley, Chichester.

Appendix II
About the Quality of Care

Assessment of physical and emotional neglect: quality of child care at home

Physical care of the child

1 Is the child appropriately dressed for the weather?
2 Is the child's clothing appropriate?
3 Is the child's clothing regularly changed?
4 Is the child washed and bathed?
5 Is hygiene at home reasonable?
6 Is a cot/pram/bed available?
7 Are sleeping arrangements appropriate?
8 Is the room warm?
9 Is safety observed, such as fire, electric points, sharp objects, medicine, chemical substances, etc.?
10 Are supervision and guidance for the child provided?
11 Is medical attention provided when the child is not well?

Nutrition

The questions below may help to assess non-organic failure-to-thrive and nutritional neglect. Failure-to-thrive assessment should also include parent–child interaction during the process of feeding and other child care activities.

1 Is the child regularly fed?
2 Is the child given enough food?
3 Is the child given appropriate food?
4 Is the child handled patiently during feeding/eating?
5 Is the child encouraged to eat?
6 Is there reasonable flexibility in feeding/eating routine?
7 Is there evidence of anger, frustration and force feeding during the feeding/eating period?
8 Is the child punished for not eating?
9 Is there awareness that the child is too thin?

10   Is there concern about the child's well-being?
11   Is there evidence of seeking help and advice?
12   Is there evidence of responding to help and advice?

From Iwaniec, D. (1995) *The Emotionally Abused and Neglected Child*
(p. 92). John Wiley, Chichester.

Appendix III

About Attachment

Observation checklist for assessing attachment

1. Birth to 1 year:

Does the child...

- Appear alert?
- Respond to humans?
- Show interest in the human face?
- Track with his eyes?
- Vocalise frequently?
- Exhibit expected motor development?
- Enjoy close physical contact?
- Exhibit discomfort?
- Appear to be easily comforted?
- Exhibit normal or excessive fussiness?
- Appear outgoing or is he passive and withdrawn?
- Have good muscle tone?
- Other:

Does the parent(s)...

- Respond to the infant's vocalisations?
- Change tone in voice when talking to the infant or about the infant?
- Show interest in face-to-face contact with the infant?
- Exhibit interest in and encourage age-appropriate development?
- Respond to the child's indications of discomfort?
- Show the ability to comfort the child?
- Enjoy close physical contact with the child?
- Initiate positive interactions with the child?
- Identify positive or negative qualities in the child that remind the parent of another family member?
- Other:

2. 1 to 5 years:

Does the child...

- Explore the environment in a normal way?
- Respond to parent(s)?
- Keep himself occupied in a positive way?
- Seem relaxed and happy?
- Have the ability to express emotions?
- React to pain and pleasure?
- Engage in age-appropriate activity?
- Use speech appropriately?
- Express frustration?
- Respond to parental limit setting?
- Exhibit observable fears?
- React positively to physical closeness?
- Respond appropriately to separation from parent?
- Respond appropriately to parent's return?
- Exhibit body rigidity or relaxation?
- Other:

3. Primary school children

Does the child...

- Behave as though he likes himself?
- Appear proud of accomplishments?
- Share?
- Perform well academically?
- Always test limits?
- Try new tasks?
- React realistically to making a mistake? Does he show fear, anger or acceptance?
- Have the ability to express emotions?
- Establish eye contact?
- Exhibit confidence in his abilities or does he frequently say 'I don't know'?
- Appear to be developing a conscience?
- Move in a relaxed way or is the body rigid?
- Feel comfortable speaking to adults?
- Smile easily?
- React to parent(s) being physically close?
- Have positive interactions with siblings and/or peers?
- Appear comfortable with his sexual identifications?
- Other:

Does the parent...

- Show interest in the child's school performance?
- Accept expression of negative feelings?
- Respond to child's overtures?
- Give support for the child in terms of developing healthy peer relationships?
- Handle problems between siblings equitably?
- Initiate affectionate disciplinary measures?
- Assign age-appropriate responsibilities to the child?
- Other:

4. Adolescents

Is the adolescent...

- Aware of his strong points?
- Aware of his weak points?
- Comfortable with his sexuality?
- Engaging in positive peer interactions?
- Performing satisfactorily in school?
- Exhibiting signs of conscience development?
- Free from severe problems with the law?
- Accepting and/or rejecting his parents' value system?
- Keeping himself occupied in appropriate ways?
- Comfortable with reasonable limits or is he constantly involved in control issues?
- Developing interests outside the home?
- Other:

Does the parent(s)...

- Set appropriate limits?
- Encourage appropriate autonomy?
- Trust the adolescent?
- Show interest in and acceptance of the adolescent's friends?
- Display interest in the adolescent's school performance?
- Exhibit interest in the adolescent's outside activities?
- Have reasonable expectations of chores and/or responsibilities adolescents should assume?
- Stand by the adolescent if he gets into trouble?
- Show affection?
- Think this child will 'turn out okay'?
- Other:

Observational checklist: long range effects of lack of normal attachment

Psychological or behavioural problems

Conscience development
- May not show normal anxiety following aggressive or cruel behaviour.
- May not show guilt on breaking the laws or rules.
- May project blame on others.

Impulse control
- Exhibits poor control; depends upon others to provide external controls on behaviour.
- Exhibits lack of foresight.
- Has a poor attention span.

Self esteem
- Is unable to get satisfaction from tasks well done.
- Sees self as undeserving.
- Sees self as incapable of change.
- Has difficulty having fun.

Interpersonal interactions
- Lacks trust in others.
- Demands affection but lacks depth in relationships.
- Exhibits hostile dependency.
- Needs to be in control of all situations.
- Has impaired social maturity.

Emotions
- Has trouble recognising own feelings.
- Has difficulty expressing feelings appropriately, especially anger, sadness and frustration.
- Has difficulty recognising feelings in others.

Cognitive problems
- Has trouble with basic cause and effect.
- Experiences problems with logical thinking.
- Appears to have confused thought processes.
- Has difficulty thinking ahead.
- May have an impaired sense of time.
- Has difficulties.

Developmental problems
- May have difficulty with auditory processing.
- May have difficulty expressing self well verbally.
- May have gross motor problems.
- May experience delays in fine motor adaptive skills.

- May experience delays in personal social development
- May have inconsistent levels of skills in all of the above areas

Checklist: ways to encourage attachment

Responding to the arousal/relaxation cycle:
- Using the child's tantrums to encourage attachment.
- Responding to the child when he is physically ill.
- Accompanying the child to doctor and dentist appointments.
- Helping the child express and cope with feelings of anger and frustration.
- Sharing the child's extreme excitement over his achievements.
- Helping the child cope with feelings about moving.
- Helping the child cope with ambivalent feelings about his birth family.
- Helping the child learn more about his past.
- Responding to a child who is hurt or injured.
- Educating the child about sexual issues.
- Other:

Initiating positive interactions
- Making affectionate overtures: hugs, kisses, physical closeness.
- Reading to the child.
- Sharing the child's 'life book'.
- Playing games.
- Going shopping together for clothes/toys for the child.
- Going on special outings: circus, plays or the like.
- Supporting the child's outside activities by providing transport or being a group leader.
- Helping the child with homework when he or she needs it.
- Teaching the child to cook or bake.
- Saying 'I love you'.
- Teaching the child about extended family members through pictures and talk.
- Helping the child understand the family 'jokes' or sayings.
- Teaching the child to participate in family activities such as bowling, camping or ski-ing.
- Helping the child meet the expectations of the other parent.
- Other:

Encouraging behaviour
- Encouraging the child to practise calling parents 'mum' and 'dad'.
- Adding a middle name to incorporate a name of family significance.
- Hanging pictures of a child on a wall.
- Involving the child in family reunions and similar activities.
- Involving the child in grandparent visits.

- Involving the child in family rituals.
- Holding religious ceremonies or other ceremonies that incorporate the child in the family.
- Buying new clothes for the child as a way of become acquainted with the child's size, colour preferences, style preferences and the like.
- Making statements such as 'in our family we do it this way' in supportive fashion.
- Sending out announcements of adoption.

Vera Fahlberg first developed this series of Checklists. Reproduced from Adcock, M. & White, R. (1985) *Good Enough Parenting: A Framework for Assessment* (p. 91) British Agencies for Adoption and Fostering.

Appendix IV

About Neglect

The attached form will take about 10 minutes to complete. It was designed to help assess the risk to children under the age of 7 years from the effects of neglectful parenting. It was anticipated that the form would be completed once an initial assessment had been completed in relation to 'neglect' referrals. The form is to be completed by the key-worker and would be completed every time the case was reviewed. By doing this, it is hoped that a more objective measure could be achieved in relation to 'good enough parenting standards' in such cases.

Experience is showing that if the form is completed after initial investigations any gaps in the investigating worker's knowledge of the family becomes readily apparent. While the form was designed to assess risk to younger children, it can still be used in relation to older children.

The higher the score, the higher the element of neglect in the family.

From Minty & Patterson (1994). This is a revised, as yet untested and unpublished, risk assessment for neglected children, building on work reported in the *British Journal of Social Work* (1994) **24**. It is reproduced here with kind permission of the authors.

Scale for Assessing Neglectful Parenting

Case No: _____

Family name(s): _____

Family composition: _____

(note ages and sex of children)

Family involved in neglect project: Yes/No

Date completed: _____

Completed by: _____

0 = Definitely untrue or never true

1 = Partially true or occasionally true

2 = Largely true or often true

3 = Definitely true or always true

NK = Not known

A *Food and eating habits*

1. There is insufficient food in the house to meet the children's needs for the next 12 hours.

    | 0 | 1 | 2 | 3 | NK |

2. Babies and toddlers are given food which is inappropriate for their age.

    | 0 | 1 | 2 | 3 | NK |

3. There are inadequate working facilities which permit meals to be prepared (e.g. cooker/stove).

    | 0 | 1 | 2 | 3 | NK |

4. There is inadequate cooking equipment (e.g. pots and pans).

    | 0 | 1 | 2 | 3 | NK |

5. The nutritional content of meals does not appear to be adequate.

    | 0 | 1 | 2 | 3 | NK |

6. Children do not have even one prepared meal per day (including school meals).

    | 0 | 1 | 2 | 3 | NK |

7. Feeding methods for young children and babies appear to be unhygienic (e.g. unsatisfactory/dirty bottles).

    | 0 | 1 | 2 | 3 | NK |

8. There is no use of fresh vegetables or fruit.

    | 0 | 1 | 2 | 3 | NK |

9. There is excessive use of sugar/sweets/crisps/chips.

    | 0 | 1 | 2 | 3 | NK |

10. There is inadequate seating for children/toddlers to have meals at the table.

    | 0 | 1 | 2 | 3 | NK |

11. Parents appear to feed babies without holding them.

    | 0 | 1 | 2 | 3 | NK |

12. Children have been observed to eat excessively/ ravenously.

    | 0 | 1 | 2 | 3 | NK |

13. Children have been reported to eat excessively/ ravenously.

    | 0 | 1 | 2 | 3 | NK |

14. Children appear to be extremely hungry.

    | 0 | 1 | 2 | 3 | NK |

15. Children are reported as extremely hungry.

    | 0 | 1 | 2 | 3 | NK |

B   Health and hygiene

16. The children look dirty. | 0 | 1 | 2 | 3 | NK |

17. The parents look dirty. | 0 | 1 | 2 | 3 | NK |

18. The home lacks showering/bathing facilities which
     work and are available for washing. | 0 | 1 | 2 | 3 | NK |

19. The bath and basin are dirty. | 0 | 1 | 2 | 3 | NK |

20. The family lacks a toilet which works.
                                                 | 0 | 1 | 2 | 3 | NK |

21. The lavatories and toilets are dirty. | 0 | 1 | 2 | 3 | NK |

22. The kitchen is dirty. | 0 | 1 | 2 | 3 | NK |

23. The kitchen equipment is unwashed. | 0 | 1 | 2 | 3 | NK |

24. Children regularly sleep in the same bed as parents.
                                                 | 0 | 1 | 2 | 3 | NK |

25. Is there a place for keeping children's clothes together
     (e.g. cupboard/drawers/basket/bag)? | 0 | 1 | 2 | 3 | NK |

26. Conditions in the parents' bedroom are much superior
     to those in the children's bedrooms. | 0 | 1 | 2 | 3 | NK |

27. Scraps of food are left on the living room/dining room
     floor. | 0 | 1 | 2 | 3 | NK |

28. Family members suffer from headlice infections.
                                                 | 0 | 1 | 2 | 3 | NK |

29. Family members have chronic scabies.
                                                 | 0 | 1 | 2 | 3 | NK |

30. There is evidence of nappy rash that is not being
     treated. | 0 | 1 | 2 | 3 | NK |

31. Children who soil/wet are left in dirty/wet clothing or
     a dirty/wet bed. | 0 | 1 | 2 | 3 | NK |

32. Parents have failed to report medical problems in their
     children (e.g. running ears, squints, recurring
     diarrhoea). | 0 | 1 | 2 | 3 | NK |

33. Parents appear to be unaware the child has a need for
     dental treatment. | 0 | 1 | 2 | 3 | NK |

34. The house has a bad smell. `0 | 1 | 2 | 3 | NK`

35. The furniture is damp. `0 | 1 | 2 | 3 | NK`

36. The garden is full of dangerous rubbish.
    `0 | 1 | 2 | 3 | NK`

C *Warmth/clothing*

37. The family lacks a heating system which works.
    `0 | 1 | 2 | 3 | NK`

38. The outside doors are badly fitted/do not work.
    `0 | 1 | 2 | 3 | NK`

39. Inside doors are left unfitted and damaged.
    `0 | 1 | 2 | 3 | NK`

40. Windows have been left unglazed/uncovered.
    `0 | 1 | 2 | 3 | NK`

41. There is no covering on the floor. `0 | 1 | 2 | 3 | NK`

42. The children have no adequate bedding (i.e. mattress
    and sheets, enough blankets or duvets).
    `0 | 1 | 2 | 3 | NK`

43. The children do not have clothes appropriate for the
    weather. `0 | 1 | 2 | 3 | NK`

44. The children have no waterproof coats.
    `0 | 1 | 2 | 3 | NK`

45. The children's shoes let in water. `0 | 1 | 2 | 3 | NK`

46. Children lack at least one set of a clean change of
    clothes. `0 | 1 | 2 | 3 | NK`

47. The children sleep in their day clothes.
    `0 | 1 | 2 | 3 | NK`

48. The bedroom window lacks curtains/blinds.
    `0 | 1 | 2 | 3 | NK`

49. The curtains are left closed all day. `0 | 1 | 2 | 3 | NK`

50. The children have clothes that do not fit them.
    `0 | 1 | 2 | 3 | NK`

51. There are insufficient nappies for all babies and toddlers who need them. ⬚ 0 | 1 | 2 | 3 | NK

52. The children's clothes smell. ⬚ 0 | 1 | 2 | 3 | NK

53. There are large holes or tears or several missing buttons/fasteners on the children's clothes. 0 | 1 | 2 | 3 | NK

54. The children's clothes are really dirty. 0 | 1 | 2 | 3 | NK

55. The children lack their own personal clothes. 0 | 1 | 2 | 3 | NK

D *Safety and supervision*

56. The children are left alone. 0 | 1 | 2 | 3 | NK

57. Babysitters are under 14 years of age. 0 | 1 | 2 | 3 | NK

58. The parents do not know the babysitters. 0 | 1 | 2 | 3 | NK

59. The child(ren) has been found wandering outside the house. 0 | 1 | 2 | 3 | NK

60. The parents do not know where young children are when they go out to play. 0 | 1 | 2 | 3 | NK

61. The children do not know where the parents are. 0 | 1 | 2 | 3 | NK

62. The parents cannot state the limits of the children's play area. 0 | 1 | 2 | 3 | NK

63. The parents allow young children to cross busy roads on their own. 0 | 1 | 2 | 3 | NK

64. For toddlers under 5 there is no safety gate which is in regular use. 0 | 1 | 2 | 3 | NK

65. If open or electric fires are used, there is no fireguard. 0 | 1 | 2 | 3 | NK

66. The children have frequent accidents involving injuries. 0 | 1 | 2 | 3 | NK

67. Windows can easily be opened by small children.

| 0 | 1 | 2 | 3 | NK |

68. Outside doors cannot be locked.

| 0 | 1 | 2 | 3 | NK |

69. Children are left in unenclosed gardens/yards.

| 0 | 1 | 2 | 3 | NK |

70. Dangerous substances are placed within young children's reach.

| 0 | 1 | 2 | 3 | NK |

71. Children are locked out of the house.

| 0 | 1 | 2 | 3 | NK |

E Emotional neglect

72. Parents hardly spend any regular time with their children.

| 0 | 1 | 2 | 3 | NK |

73. Parents do not play with their children.

| 0 | 1 | 2 | 3 | NK |

74. There are no regular bed times for children.

| 0 | 1 | 2 | 3 | NK |

75. Under 8s are still up at 10.00 PM.

| 0 | 1 | 2 | 3 | NK |

76. When children are distressed parents do not comfort them.

| 0 | 1 | 2 | 3 | NK |

77. The parents have very unrealistic expectations of their children's abilities.

| 0 | 1 | 2 | 3 | NK |

78. The parents expect their children to look after themselves.

| 0 | 1 | 2 | 3 | NK |

79. The parents are quite unable to control small children.

| 0 | 1 | 2 | 3 | NK |

80. The parents respond insensitively to their children's needs.

| 0 | 1 | 2 | 3 | NK |

81. The children are indiscriminately affectionate to strangers.

| 0 | 1 | 2 | 3 | NK |

82. The children do not turn appropriately to other adults.

| 0 | 1 | 2 | 3 | NK |

83. The parents have at best only a dim awareness of their children and their needs.

| 0 | 1 | 2 | 3 | NK |

84. The parents' response to their children's behaviour appears to be very unpredictable. `0` `1` `2` `3` `NK`

85. Parents largely leave the children to their own devices. `0` `1` `2` `3` `NK`

86. Parents are violent in front of their children. `0` `1` `2` `3` `NK`

87. Parents frequently argue in front of their children. `0` `1` `2` `3` `NK`

88. Parents frequently argue when their children are in the house, but out of sight. `0` `1` `2` `3` `NK`

89. The parents have made suicide attempts in front of their children. `0` `1` `2` `3` `NK`

90. The parents have made suicide threats in front of their children. `0` `1` `2` `3` `NK`

91. The parents have threatened to leave the children or put them into care if they do not behave. `0` `1` `2` `3` `NK`

92. Frequently no action is taken to check bad and/or dangerous behaviour. `0` `1` `2` `3` `NK`

93. Children are not encouraged to care for their toys. `0` `1` `2` `3` `NK`

94. The parents appear to set no limit to TV watching. `0` `1` `2` `3` `NK`

95. A parent fails to show pride in their child's achievement. `0` `1` `2` `3` `NK`

96. Mother/father cannot show physical affection to the child/children. `0` `1` `2` `3` `NK`

97. Children are not encouraged to paint or draw or play constructively. `0` `1` `2` `3` `NK`

98. Children have no books of their own. `0` `1` `2` `3` `NK`

99. Children have no age-appropriate toys, dolls. `0` `1` `2` `3` `NK`

100. Parents do not teach their children the difference between right or wrong in a manner appropriate to their level of development. | 0 | 1 | 2 | 3 | NK |

101. The parents buy themselves expensive clothes, jewels, consumer goods, but provide hardly anything for the children. | 0 | 1 | 2 | 3 | NK |

102. Bullying or cruelty by older siblings to younger siblings goes unchecked. | 0 | 1 | 2 | 3 | NK |

103. Children are locked in bedrooms, cupboards. | 0 | 1 | 2 | 3 | NK |

104. Dangerous animals are left insufficiently controlled. | 0 | 1 | 2 | 3 | NK |

105. The animals appear better fed and cared for than the children. | 0 | 1 | 2 | 3 | NK |

106. Spiteful or cruel play with pets goes unchecked. | 0 | 1 | 2 | 3 | NK |

107. The house or garden/yard is frequently fouled with animal faeces/urine. | 0 | 1 | 2 | 3 | NK |

F   *School*

108. Parents regularly withdraw their children from school\nursery. | 0 | 1 | 2 | 3 | NK |

109. Children regularly turn up late for school/nursery. | 0 | 1 | 2 | 3 | NK |

110. School age children are regularly not provided with an adequate lunch or dinner money. | 0 | 1 | 2 | 3 | NK |

111. Infant/nursery children make their own way to school/nursery by themselves. | 0 | 1 | 2 | 3 | NK |

Do not score this section

| YES | NO |

a. Parents report feeding difficulties with a child.

| | |

b. Feeding problems are observed in relation to a particular child.

| | |

c.   Children have been observed to eat excessively slowly. $\boxed{|}$

d.   Children have been reported to eat excessively slowly. $\boxed{|}$

C1

a.   The families can afford to pay for their heating systems. $\boxed{|}$

b.   There are serious structural deficiencies in the house (e.g. rotten floor boards, leaking roof). $\boxed{|}$

c.   The house is unusually damp. $\boxed{|}$

Appendix V

About Negative Parental Feelings

Chain of damaging thoughts, negative feelings, and unhappy outcomes

Event	Belief	Feeling	Behaviour	Outcome
Child fails to thrive.	I cannot cope. He/she deliberately behaves like that to hurt me.	Inadequacy, helplessness, despair.	Force feeding, screaming shouting, frustration, anxiety.	Food avoidance behaviour, losing weight.
Developmental delays.	He/she dislikes being picked up or talked to. Dislikes me.	Depression, frustration, uselessness.	Do nothing.	Child is under stimulated. Emotional neglect.
Child does not respond to parental requests (oppositional behaviour).	I am inadequate as a parent. I cannot cope.	Frustration, anger, depression.	Smacks, shouts, criticises.	Distorted relationship. Emotional abuse.

From Iwaniec, D. (1995) *The Emotionally Abused and Neglected Child* (p. 113). John Wiley, Chichester.

Appendix VI

About Predicting Quality of Care in Parents with Learning Difficulties

Predicting adequacy/inadequacy of parenting/child care

Predicting adequacy of parenting

Initial and ongoing maternal outcomes:

1. Maternal knowledge and skill in:
   (a) healthcare: healthcare, safety, responding to emergencies.
   (b) child stimulatory behaviour: for adequate child cognitive, emotional and social status and development.
   (c) dealing with child behaviour problems and disciplining children.

Process variables associated with adequate acquisition, maintenance, generalisation and development of the above variables, including:

1. Rapidity with which the mother learns new material and unlearns old behaviours (e.g. using punishment all the time).
2. How well she makes decisions.
3. How well she solves problems.
4. How well she copes with/adapts to new situations.

Initial child outcomes:

1. Current cognitive development.
2. Current emotional development, effect.
3. Current physical development (e.g. head circumference, body weight).
4. Current health status (e.g. immunisations up to date, illnesses, accidents).

Ongoing child outcomes.

1. Rate at which development occurs in the above areas.
2. Adequacy of health at each developmental stage.
3. Ultimate levels attained.

Factors associated with:

Inadequacy of parenting	Adequacy of parenting

Historical
(a) Environmental

Ever institutionalised?	
In special education?	Lived with own parents?

(b) Familial

Abused as a child?	Having appropriate parent role?
One or both parents with LD, a medical problem or engaged in criminal activity	Models?

(c) Maternal

Presence of lifelong medical or emotional disorder?	Adequate maternal physical and emotional health?
Negative attitude towards parenting?	

Current
(a) Environmental support

Income below poverty level?	Adequate income?
Inadequate support agencies, including untrained staff, involvement with multiple agencies?	Adequate resources, supports? Willingness to use supports?

(b) Familial

No parenting models?	Supportive, healthy partner?
No parental support?	Marital harmony?
Partner with emotional disorder, abusive or with medical disorder?	

(c) Child

More than one child?	Only one healthy child?
Child over 6 years?	
Child with medical and/or behaviour problem and/or difficult temperament?	

(d) Maternal

Emotional disturbance as well as LD?	Absence of additional problems?
High stress level?	
Poor self esteem?	
IQ below 60	IQ above 60?
Poor reading recognition and comprehension (below grade 4)?	Adequate education and skills?
Limited or no parenting knowledge or skills?	Maternal knowledge and skills *re*: health, safety, emergencies, child stimulation, management of behaviour?
Medical problems as well as LD?	
Poor decision making, coping and problem solving?	
Punitive, authoritarian, non-empathic?	

Based on Tymchuk, A (1992) Predicting adequacy of parenting by people with mental retardation. *Child Abuse and Neglect*, **16**, 165–78.

Appendix VII

Making Links Between Theory and Practice (Nottinghamshire Social Services Department)

Child in need: level two assessment part C

NAME OF CHILD	DoB

This form should be completed **for each child who is included in a Level Two assessment** (and a written report for ICPC should include a summary of this information). Workers may need to seek involvement of other professionals or teams in order to gather information.

ALL SECTIONS MUST BE CONSIDERED FOR RELEVANCE AND COMPLETED. QUESTIONS SHOULD BE INTERPRETED IN RELATION TO THE AGE AND ABILITY OF THE CHILD.

DETAIL MUST BE GIVEN TO SUPPORT RESPONSE

C1 HEALTH	
	Supporting comment and information, including any comments by parents or child/young person
1. Is the child/young person normally well? ☐ Yes ☐ No ☐ Has health/medical condition which affects their well being	
2. Does the child have disability? ☐ Yes ☐ No	
3. Are there any concerns for the growth and/or development of the child/young person? ☐ Yes ☐ No	

4. In relation to Q 1, 2 and 3 are any concerns/conditions being addressed?

☐   Yes appropriate action
     being taken
☐   None or limited action

5. Is there any risk to the child/young person's health (e.g. self harming behaviour, substance use/misuse, eating disorders, failure to protect by carers)?

☐   Yes
☐   No

Any particular concerns/actions to be considered for a plan

C2   EDUCATION

Preschool/nursery child

1. Does the child receive and respond to the stimulation of their parent/carer according to their age and ability?

☐   Yes
☐   No

2. Does the child actively explore their environment at home?

☐   Yes
☐   No

3. Are the child's communication skills developing satisfactorily for their age and ability?

☐   Yes
☐   No

4. Does the child have the opportunity to play with similar age children within the family network or in a group setting?

☐   Yes
☐   No

School age child

Name of School   Tel No.

Year of next school move

5. Is the child's/young person's (educational) attainment average for their age?

☐   Yes
☐   No

6. Are there any concerns about the child/young person's attendance?

□ Yes
□ No

7. Does the child/young person have any identified special educational needs (e.g. SEN)?

□ Yes | Identify support given
□ No

8. Is any action being taken to plan for the young person's future (e.g. Transition planning (SEN children), D P Act assessment, career/FE guidance)?

□ Yes
□ No

Any particular concerns/actions to be considered for a plan

C3 IDENTITY

1. Does the child have access to positive images of similar children/young persons (consider race, gender, sexuality, disability, age)?

□ Yes
□ No

2. Does the child have an understanding of their ethnic and cultural background?

□ Yes
□ No

3. Does the child understand their personal history (consider knowledge of extended family members and child's history)?

□ Yes
□ No

4. Does the child/young person express positive views about themselves and their abilities?

□ Yes
□ No

Any particular concerns/actions to be considered for a plan

C4 FAMILY AND SOCIAL RELATIONSHIPS

1. Has the child/young person had continuity of carers?

☐ Yes
☐ No

2. Is the child/young person attached to at least one care giver?

☐ Yes
☐ No

3. Does the child/young person make and sustain friendships with others of their age?

☐ Yes
☐ No

4. Does the child/young person generally make positive relationships with others (e.g. other adults, wider community)?

☐ Yes
☐ No

Any particular concerns/actions to be considered for a plan

C5 SOCIAL PRESENTATION

1. Does the child/young person look well cared for (i.e. personal hygiene, clothing)?

☐ Yes
☐ No

2. Is the child's/young person's behaviour acceptable to others?

☐ Yes
☐ No

3. Is the child/young person able to make themselves understood?

☐ Yes
☐ No

Any particular concerns/actions to be considered for a plan

C6 EMOTIONAL AND BEHAVIOURAL DEVELOPMENT

If there are concerns in this area – you should consider using the relevant age appropriate Good Parenting Assessment and Action Record for guidance for a more detailed assessment.

1. Does the child/young person have any emotional and behavioural difficulties?

☐ Yes
☐ No

2. Is the child/young person receiving effective help for any difficulties (record who is working for the child)?

☐ Yes
☐ No

Any particular concerns/actions to be considered for a plan

C7 SELF CARE SKILLS

1. Is the child/young person learning self care skills?

☐ Yes
☐ No

Any particular concerns/actions to be considered for a plan

Information sources for assessment

Has this assessment been shared with the child/
young person?

Yes/No

By whom ....

Date(s) ....

Has this assessment been shared with the
child's/young persons parents or carers?

Yes/No

By whom ....

Date(s) ....

Date Form C completed ....

Signatures:

Signature: Designation: Date:

Any actions to address particular needs of the child/young person, that have been identified or agreed with the parents or carers should be transferred to the Plan (CH/CIN/3/PLAN) for the child.

Appendix VIII

Leverhulme Workshop on Neglect

Nottingham participants 1997

Ms Vicky Bailey	Nurse Manager
Mr Nigel Bennett	Principal Officer Operations/Barnados
Ms Anne Court	Educational and Forensic Psychologist
Dr Liz Didcock	Community Paediatrician
Dr Helen Earwicker	General Practitioner
Ms Sara Glennie	Visiting Lecturer in Social Work
Mrs Debbie Hindle	Principal Child Psychotherapist
Dr Yossi Korazim	Ministry of Labour Social Affairs/ Jerusalem
Dr Rachel Lehup	Child Psychiatrist
Dr Yin Ng	Consultant Paediatrician
Ms Carol Pattinson	Service Manager/Children and Families/ Social Services
Ms Jill Pedley	Service Manager/Social Services
Ms Mary Perry	Policy Officer/Social Services
Ms Dori Rivkin	Researcher Centre for Children and Youth/ Jerusalem
Mrs Sandy Rowles	Child Protection Advisor/Health
Mr Dave Seal	Principal Officer Child Protection/Social Services
Ms Alison Shield	Child Protection Coordinator/Social Services
Mr David Spicer	Barrister
Prof Olive Stevenson	Emeritus Professor of Social Work Studies
Prof June Thoburn	Professor of Social Work
Dr Jane Tresidder	Community Paediatrician

Oxford participants 1997

Mr Peter Clark	Joint Head of Legal Services
Dr Danya Glaser	Child/Adolescent Psychiatrist
Ms Sara Glennie	Visiting Lecturer in Social Work

Dr Mary Hamill	Community Paediatrician
Mrs Ann Head	*Guardian Ad Litem*
Ms Ruth Jutkowski	Division of Youth and Families/Jerusalem
Dr Margaret Lynch	Reader in Community Paediatrics
Mr Sam Monaghan	Principal Officer/Child Protection/Social Services
Ms Ruth Nissim	Principal Psychologist
Ms Alyson Packham	Nurse Facilitator Child Protection
Ms Jayne Paterson	Staff Development Officer/Social Services
Ms Julie Selwyn	Lecturer University Centre for Family Policy
Ms Gill Steckiewicz	Unit Manager/Social Services
Prof Olive Stevenson	Emeritus Professor of Social Work Studies
Mr Bill Stone	Child Protection Social Worker/NSPCC
Ms Maureen Thompson	Senior Social Work Practitioner/Social Services
Dr Harriet Ward	Senior Lecturer

Appendix IX

Looking after Children:
Research into Practice

The following titles are published by HMSO:

Looking After Children: ISBN 0 11 321846 X (1995)
Management and Implementation Guide

Looking After Children: ISBN 0 11 321459 6 (1991)
Assessing Outcomes in Child Care

Looking After Children: ISBN 0 11 321845 1 (1995)
Good Parenting, Good Outcomes Training Resources Pack

Looking After Children: ISBN 0 11 321847 8 (1995)
Research into Practice

Looking After Children: ISBN 0 11 321903 2 (1995)
Trial Pack

Looking After Children: ISBN 0 11 321884 2 (1995)
Training Guide

Looking After Children: ISBN 0 11 321849 4 (1995)
Essential Information Record

Looking After Children: ISBN 0 11 321850 8 (1995)
Placement Plan

Looking After Children: ISBN 0 11 321848 6 (1995)
Review

Looking After Children: ISBN 0 11 321851 6 (1995)
Care Plan

Looking After Children: ISBN 0 11 321852 4 (1995)
Consultation Papers

Assessment and Action Records: ISBN 0 11 321854 0 (1995)
Under 1 year

Assessment and Action Records: ISBN 0 11 321855 9 (1995)
1 and 2 years

Assessment and Action Records: ISBN 0 11 321856 7 (1995)
3 and 4 years

Assessment and Action Records: ISBN 0 11 321857 5 (1995)
5–9 years

Assessment and Action Records: ISBN 0 11 321858 3 (1995)
10–14 years

Assessment and Action Records: ISBN 0 11 321859 1 (1995)
15 years and over

References

Adcock, M. & White, R. (1985) *Good Enough Parenting*. British Agencies for Adoption and Fostering, London.

Aldgate, J. & Simmonds, J. (1988) *Direct Work with Children*. Batsford, London.

Aldgate, J., Bradley, M. & Hawley, D. (1996) Respite accommodation: a case study of partnership under The Children Act 1989. pp. 147–169. In *Child Welfare Services*, (eds M. Hill, & J. Aldgate). Jessica Kingsley, London.

Allen, R. & Oliver, J. (1982) The effects of child maltreatment on language development. *Child Abuse and Neglect*, 6, 299–305.

Allsopp, M. & Stevenson, O. (1995) Social workers' perceptions of risk in child protection. ESRC project. (A discussion paper.) Nottingham University.

Baird, S. & Neufeldt, D. (1988) Assessing potential for abuse and neglect. *National Council on Crime and Delinquency Focus*.

Becker, S. (1997) *Responding to Poverty*. Longman, Harlow.

Beckford, Jasmine: *A child in trust* (1985) Report of the Panel of Inquiry into the circumstances surrounding the death of Jasmine Beckford. Presented to Brent Borough Council and to Brent Health Authority.

Belsky, J. & Vondra, J. (1989) Lessons from child abuse: the determinants of parenting. In *Child Maltreatment* (eds D. Cicchetti & V. Carlson). Cambridge University Press, Cambridge.

Birchall, E. & Hallett, C. (1995) *Working Together in Child Protection. Studies in Child Protection*. HMSO, London.

Blackburn, C. (1991) *Poverty & Health. Working with Families*. Open University Press, Buckingham.

Blaxter, M. & Patterson, E. (1984) *Mothers and Daughters, Studies in Deprivation and Disadvantage*. Heinemann, London.

Booth, T. & Booth, W. (1993) Parenting with learning difficulties: lessons with practitioners. *British Journal of Social Work*, 23, (5) 459–80.

Bowlby, J. (1969, 1973, 1980) *Attachment and Loss*, Vols I, II, III. Hogarth Press, London. (Editions from 1951 onwards.)

The Bridge Consultancy (1995) *Paul: Death Through Neglect*. The Bridge Consultancy Services, London.

Bridge, G. & Miles, M. (eds) (1996) *On the Outside looking in. Collected Essays on Young Child Observation in Social Work Training*. Central Council for Education and Training in Social Work, London.

Channer, Y. & Parton, P. (1990) Racism, cultural relativism and child protection. In *Violence against Children Study Group. Taking Child Abuse Seriously*, pp. 105–20. Unwin, London and New York.

Charles, M., Kingaby, D. & Thorn J. (1996) *Fun and families*. Report of Nottingham Area Child Protection Committee. (Report available from: M Charles, Lecturer in Social Work, School of Social Studies, Nottingham University, NG7 4RD.)

Collins, G. & Nicholson. J. (1997) *Parents with learning disabilities: a survey of current service involvement in the Nottinghamshire area.* Unpublished report for multi agency working party on parents with learning disabilities, Central Nottinghamshire Healthcare Trust and Nottinghamshire Social Services Department.

Coohey, C. (1995) Neglectful mothers, their mothers and partners: the significance of mutual aid. *Child Abuse and Neglect*, **19**, (8) 885–95.

Cooper, C. (1985) 'Good enough', border line and 'bad enough parenting'. In *Good Enough Parenting*, (eds M. Adcock & R. White), pp. 58–80. British Agencies for Adoption and Fostering, London.

Creighton, S. (1986) *NSPCC Research Briefing*, No 5, August.

Crittenden, P. (1988) Family dyadic patterns of functioning in maltreating families. In *Early Predicting and Prevention of Child Abuse*, (eds K. Browne, C. Davies & P. Strattan), pp. 161–89. Wiley, London and New York.

Crittenden, P. (1992) Children's strategies for coping with adverse home environments: an interpretation using attachment theory. *Child Abuse and Neglect*, **16**, 329–43.

Crittenden, P. (1993) An information processing perspective on the behaviour of neglectful parents. *Criminal Justice and Behaviour*, **20**, (1) 27–48.

Crouch, J. & Milner, J. (1993) Effects of child neglect on children. *Criminal Justice and Behaviour*, **20** (1).

Daro, D. (1988) *Confronting Child Abuse*. New York Free Press, New York.

Department of Health (1988) *Protecting Children: A Guide for Social Workers undertaking a Comprehensive Assessment*. HMSO, London.

Department of Health (1989) *Working Together*. HMSO, London.

Department of Health (1991) *Child Abuse: A Study of Inquiry Reports 1980–1989*. HMSO, London.

Department of Health (1994) *The Child, the Court and the Video*. Social Services Inspectorate Health Publications Unit, Manchester.

Department of Health (1997) *Children's Service News*, July.

DHSS (1974) *Report of the Committee of Inquiry into the Care and Supervision provided in relation to Maria Colwell*. HMSO, London.

Dingwall, R. Ekelaar, J. & Murray, T. (1983, 1995) *The Protection of Children*. Avebury, Basingstoke.

Dutt, R. & Phillips, M. (1996) Race, culture and the prevention of child abuse. In submission to Commission of Inquiry into the prevention of child abuse. *Childhood Matters*, **2**, 154–96.

Egeland, B. (1988a) The consequences of physical and emotional neglect on the development of young children. *Research symposium on child neglect*. Washington DC.

Egeland, B. (1988b) Breaking the cycle of abuse: implications for prediction and intervention. In *Early Prediction and Prevention of Child Abuse*, (eds K. Bourne *et al.*). John Wiley, London and New York.

Egeland, B. & Sroufe, A. (1981) Developmental sequelae of maltreatment in infancy. In *New Directions for Child Development*, (eds R. Rizley & D. Cicchetti). pp. 77–92. Jossey Bass, San Francisco.

Egeland, B., Sroufe, A. & Erikson, M. (1983) The developmental consequences of different patterns of maltreatment. *Child Abuse and Neglect*, 7, 459–69.

Farmer, E. & Owen, M. (1995) *Child Protection Practice: Private Risks and Public Remedies*. HMSO, London.

Finch, J. (1989) *Family Obligations and Social Change*. Cambridge Policy Press, London.

Fox, S. & Dingwall, R. (1988) An exploratory study of variations in social workers' and health visitors' definitions of child maltreatment. *British Journal of Social Work*, 5, (5) 467–77.

Fox, L., Long, S. & Langlois, A. (1988) Patterns of language comprehension deficit in abused and neglected children. *Journal of Speech and Hearing Disorders*, 53, 239–44.

Freud, A., Solnit, A. & Goldstein, J. (1973) *Beyond the Best Interests of the Child*. The Free Press, New York.

Frost, N., Johnston, E., Stein, M. & Wallis, L. (1997) *Negotiated Friendship*. Home-Start, Leicester.

Fuller, R. & Stevenson, O. (1983) *Policies, Programmes and Disadvantage*. Heinemann, London.

Gaudin, J. (1993) *Child Neglect: A Guide for Intervention*. National Center on Child Abuse and Neglect (US Department of Health and Human Services).

Gaudin, J. & Polansky, N. (1986) Distancing of the neglectful family. *Children and Youth Services Review*, 8, 1–12.

Giavannoni, J. & Becarra, R. (1979) *Defining Child Abuse*. New York Free Press, New York.

Gibbons, J., Conroy, S. & Bell, C. (1993) *Operation of child protection registers*. Report to the Department of Health. University of East Anglia.

Gibbons, J., Thorpe, S. & Wilkinson, P. (1990) *Family Support and Prevention. Studies in Local Areas*. HMSO, London.

Glaser, D. & Prior, V. (1997) Is the term child protection applicable to emotional abuse? *Child Abuse Review*, 6, 315–29.

Glendinning., C. & Millar, J. (eds) (1992) *Women and Poverty in Britain: The 1990s*. Harvester Wheatsheaf, London and New York.

Glennie, S. & Hendry, E. (eds) (1996) *Promoting Quality: Standards for Interagency Child Protection Training*. PIAT (Promoting interagency training). NSPCC/PIAT, London.

Goldberg, M., Gibbons, J. & Sinclair, I. (1985) *Problems, Tasks and Outcomes: The Evaluation of Task Centred Casework in Three Settings*. Allen and Unwin, London.

Goldstein, J., Solnit, J., Goldstein, S. & the late Anna Freud (1996) *The Best Interests of the Child*. The Free Press, New York.

Gough, D. (1993) The case for and against prevention. In *Child Abuse and Child Abusers* (Research Highlights in Social Work 24, (ed. L. Waterhouse). pp. 208–52. Jessica Kingsley, London and Philadelphia.

Graham, H. (1992) Budgeting for Health: mothers in low income households. In *Women and Poverty in Britain: The 1990s*, (eds C. Glendinning & J. Millar). Harvester Wheatsheaf, London and New York.

Hackett, L. & Hackett, R. (1994) Child rearing practices and psychiatric disorder in Gujurati and British children. *British Journal of Social Work*, 24, 191–202.

Hallett, C. (1995) *Interagency Coordination in Child Protection*. HMSO, London.

Hallett, C. & Stevenson, O. (1980) *Child Abuse: Aspects of Interprofessional Cooperation*. Allen & Unwin, London.

Hardiker, P., Exton, K. & Barker, M. (1991a) *Policies & Practices in Preventive Child Care*. Gower, Avebury.

Hardiker, P., Exton, K. & Barker M. (1991b) The social policy contexts of prevention in child care. *British Journal of Social Work*, **21**, 341–60.

Hill, M. & Laing, P. (1979) *Social Work and Money*. Allen and Unwin, London.

Howe, D. (1992) Child abuse and the bureaucratisation of social work. *Sociological Review*, **38**, 491–508.

Howe, D. (1995) *Attachment Theory for Social Work Practice*. McMillan, Basingstoke.

Howe, D. (1996) Surface and depth in social work practice. In *Social Theory, Social Change and Social Work*, (ed. N. Parton). Routledge, London.

Howe, D. (1997) *Patterns of Adoption*. Blackwell Science Ltd, Oxford.

Huby, M. & Dix, G. (1992) *Evaluating the Social Fund. Research Report No 9*. Department of Social Security. HMSO, London.

Iwaniec, D. (1995) *The Emotionally Abused and Neglected Child*. John Wiley, Chichester.

Jehu, D., Yelloly, M. & Shaw, M. (1972) *Behaviour Modification in Social Work*. Wiley and Sons, London and New York.

Jones, J. & McNeely, (1980) Mothers who neglect and those who do not: a comparative study. *Journal of Contemporary Social Work*, 424–31.

Kahn, A. & Kammerman, S. (1996) *Beyond: beyond the best interests....* Paper presented in November 1996 at the Hebrew University of Jerusalem at an international conference.

Kempe, C. & Helfer, R. (1968) *The Battered Child*. Chicago University Press, Chicago.

Korbin, J. (1991) Cross cultural perspectives and research directions for the 21st century. *Child Abuse and Neglect*, **15**(Suppl. 1), 67–77.

Kurtz, P., Gaudin, J., Wardaski, J. & Howing, P. (1993a) Maltreatment and the school aged child: school performance consequences. *Child Abuse and Neglect*, **17**, 581–9.

Kurtz, P., Gaudin, J., Howing, P. & Wodarski, J. (1993b) The consequences of physical abuse and neglect on the school age child. *Children and Youth Services Review*, **15**, 85–104.

Lynch, M. & Stevenson, O. (1990) Fox, Stephanie: *Report of the Practice Review*. Commissioned by the Wandsworth Child Protection Committee.

McGaw, S. (undated) *I Want to be a Good Parent*. Bild Publications, Kidderminster.

McGaw, S. & Sturmey, P. (1994) Assessing parents with learning disabilities: the parental skills model. *Child Abuse Review*, **3**, (1) 27–35.

McGlone, F., Park, A. & Roberts, C. (1996). Relative values: kinship and friendship. *British Social Attitudes: 13th Report*, pp. 53–72. Dartmouth Publishing Company, Dartmouth.

Magistrates Association (1994) *The welfare of the child. Assessing evidence in children's cases*. The Learning Business.

Maher, P. (1987) *Child Abuse: The Educational Perspective*. Blackwell Publishers, Oxford.

Maitra, B. (1995) Giving due consideration to the family's racial and cultural background. In *Assessment of Parenting*, (eds P. Reder & C. Lucey), pp. 151–68. Routledge, London and New York.

Marsh, P. & Crow, G. (1997) *Family Group Conferences*. Blackwell Science Ltd, Oxford.

Mass, M. (1996) The need for a paradigm shift in social work: the study of parenting 5. *Journal for Theory of Social Behaviour*, 26, 425.

Mattinson, J. & Sinclair, I. (1979) Mate and Stalemate. Blackwell Publishers, Oxford.

Minty, B. & Patterson, G. (1994) The nature of child neglect. *British Journal of Social Work*, 24, 733–48.

Ney, P., Fung, T. & Wickett, A. (1994) The worst combination of child abuse and neglect. *Child Abuse and Neglect*, 18, 9, 705–14.

Oppenheim, C. & Harker, L. (1996) *Poverty: The Facts*. Child Poverty Action Group, London.

Owusa-Bempah, K. (forthcoming 1998) The relevance of confidentiality in social work practice across two cultures. In *Social Work Processes*, (eds B. Compton & B. Galaway), 5th edn. Brooks Cole, Pacific Grove, California.

Parker, G. (1992) Making ends meet: women credit and debt. In *Women and Poverty in Britain: The 1990s*, (eds C. Glendinning & J. Millar). Harvester Wheatsheaf, London and New York.

Parton, N. (1985) *The Politics of Child Abuse*. Macmillan, London and New York.

Philp, F. (1963) *Family Failure*. Faber and Faber, London.

Pianti, R. Egeland, B. & Erikson, M. (1989) The antecedants of maltreatment. *Child Maltreatment*, (eds D. Cicchetti & V. Carlson). Cambridge University Press, Cambridge.

Platt, S., Martin, C., Hunt, J. *et al.* (1989) Damp housing, mould growth and symptomatic health state. *British Medical Journal*, 298, 1673–8.

Polansky, N. (1981) Childhood level of living scale. In *An Anatomy of Neglect*, (eds N. Polansky, M. Chalmers, E. Butterweiser, & D. Williams). Chicago University Press, Chicago.

Polansky, N., Ammons, P. & Gaudin, J. (1985a) Loneliness and isolation in child neglect. *Social Casework*, 38–48.

Polansky, N., Chalmers, M.A., Butterweiser, E. & Williams, D. (1981) *An Anatomy of Neglect*. Chicago University Press, Chicago.

Polansky, N., Gaudin, J., Ammons, P. & Davis, K. (1985b) The psychological ecology of the neglectful mother. *Child Abuse and Neglect*, 9, 265–75.

Pound, A. (1994) *Newpin – a Befriending and Therapeutic Network for Carers of Young Children*. HMSO, London.

Rashid, S. (1996) Attachment viewed through a cultural lens. In *Attachment and Loss in Child and Family Social Work*, (ed. D. Howe), pp. 59–81. Avebury, Basingstoke..

Robertson, J. & Robertson, J. (1953) *A two year old goes to hospital* (film). Ipswich concord films council.

Robertson, J. & Robertson, J. (1969) *John: 17 months: nine days at a residential nursery* (film). Ipswich concord films council.

Robinson, C. (1996) Research review: short term care for children. *Child and Family Social Work*, 1.4, 261–6.

Rutter, M. (1967) A children's behaviour questionnaire for completion by teachers. *Journal of Child Psychology and Psychiatry*, 8, 1–11.

Rutter, M. (1968) The reliability and validity of the psychiatric assessment of the child. *British Journal of Psychiatry*, 114, 563–79.

Rutter, M. (1991) A fresh look at maternal deprivation. In *The Development and Integration of Behaviour*, (ed. P. Bateson). Cambridge University Press, Cambridge.

Rutter, M. & Rutter, M. (1993) *Developing Minds: Challenge and Continuity across the Life Span*. Penguin Books, Harmondsworth.

Savage, M. (1994) Can early indications of neglecting families be observed? *Child Care in Practice*, 27–38.

Seagull, E. (1987) Social support and child maltreatment: a review of the evidence. *Child Abuse and Neglect*, 11, 41–52.

Sheldon, B. (1986) Social work effectiveness experiments: review and implications. *British Journal of Social Work*, 16, 223–42.

Skuse, D.H. (1985) Non organic failure to thrive: a reappraisal. *Archives of Diseases in Childhood*, 20, 173–8.

Smith, C. & Pugh, G. (1996) Learning to be a parent: a survey of group based parenting programmes. (Family and Parenthood. Policy and Practice). National Childrens Bureau, London. (Contains addresses for information on group parenting programmes.)

Social Security Advisory Committee (1997) *Social Security (Lone Parent) (Amendment) Regulations*. Cm 3713. The Stationery Office, London.

Social Services Inspectorate (1994) *The Child, the Court and the Video*. Department of Health, London.

Stevenson, O. (1970) *Claimant or Client?* Routledge Kegan Paul, London.

Stevenson, O. (1989) Multi disciplinary work in child protection. In *Child Abuse Public Policy and Professional Practice*, pp. 173–203. Harvester Wheatsheaf, London and New York.

Stevenson, O. (1995) Case conferences in child protection. In *The Child Protection Handbook*, (eds K. Wilson & A. James), pp. 227–41. Bailliere Tindall, London and New York.

Stevenson, O. (1996) Emotional abuse and neglect: a time for reappraisal. *Child and Family Social Work*, 1, (1) 13–18.

Thoburn, J., Lewis, A. Shemmings, D. (1995) *Paternalism or Partnership? Family Involvement in the Child Protection Process*. HMSO, London.

Thoburn, J., Brandon, M., Lewis, A. & Way, A. (1996) *Safeguarding children with The Children Act 1989*. School of Social Work, University of East Anglia.

Titmuss, R. (1971) Welfare rights, law and discretion. *Political Quarterly*, 42.2, 113–132.

Townsend, P., Davidson, N. & Whitehead, M. (1988) *Inequalities in Health*. Penguin Books, London.

Trowell, J. & Bower, H. (1995) *The Emotional Needs of Young Children and their Families*. Routledge, London and New York.

Ward, H. (1995) *Looking after Children: Research into Practice. Second Report to Department of Health*. HMSO, London.

White, Leanne: *Report of Overview Group into the circumstances surrounding the death of Leanne White*. (1994) Nottinghamshire Area Child Protection Committee.

Wilding, J. & Thoburn, J. (1997) Family support plans for neglected and emotionally maltreated children. *Child Abuse Review*, 6.

Wilson, B. (1993) *The use of section one payments by social workers. A study of influences and outcome of decisions.* PhD Thesis, University of Brighton.

Zuragin, S. (1988) Child abuse, child neglect and maternal depression: is there a connection? *Research Symposium on Child Neglect.* Washington DC.

Index